Glory

The Holiness of God and Man

Dr. Charles R. Vogan Jr.

***Cover photo by Bryan Johnson,* www.trekearth.com**

ISBN 978-0-6151-5619-4

Ravenbrook Publishers

A subsidiary of
Shenandoah Bible Ministries

www.shenbible.org

1 2 **3**

Contents

Introduction

Now this is eternal life: that they may know you, the only true God, and Jesus Christ, whom you have sent. (John 17:3)

Life has a sinister way of diverting us from our true course.

Man was made for the sole purpose of knowing and serving God. But we have strayed so far away from that purpose that many people actually think this idea of living for God alone is strange. They didn't know that there *was* anything in God to get excited about. They thought that the purpose of life here was – well, to enjoy themselves. The world is full of things to enjoy, and opportunities for the good life abound. The only time they actually think of God is when they get in trouble, and they need someone bigger than they are to pull them out.

There are a few people in history, however, who have stepped through the veil of this world into the world of God and discovered *pure joy*. There's a difference between knowing about God and actually meeting him face to face. Those privileged few wouldn't trade the experience for anything in this world. Paul stated it best:

> I must go on boasting. Although there is nothing to be gained, I will go on to visions and revelations from the Lord. I know a man in Christ who fourteen years ago was caught up to the third heaven. Whether it was in the body or out of the body I do not know – God knows. And I know that this man – whether in the body or apart from the body I do not know, but God knows – was caught up to paradise. He heard inexpressible things,

things that man is not permitted to tell. (2 Corinthians 12:1-4)

Obviously Paul wants to go to Heaven and live with God. So do all who have "tasted and seen that God is good." Unfortunately few have this desire; most are quite satisfied with this world, and they have no interest in God. The problem is that you *have* to leave this world behind to find God.

Ironically this attitude pervades the Church as well. So-called "Christians" are content to talk about God, but make no effort to seek and find God for themselves. Like Lot's wife, they also love this world too much to leave it.

We can't force people to get interested in God. And it will prove impossible to talk many people out of the "good things" of this world that they hold so precious. But the fact remains that we have ample warning in the Bible that those good things will only last for so long – the day is coming when it will all be stripped away, ripped forcibly out of our hands (either through death or the terror of the Last Day), and we will be naked and helpless before God the Judge. If at that point we have not yet found God to be our only delight, he will turn out to be our eternal terror. God will not be trifled with. *Now* is the day of salvation; now is our opportunity to find God, before the Day of Judgment when God will examine the heart of every human being and determine where their love really lies.

What we want to do in this study is turn our eyes toward God, and see if what the Bible says about him is really true. Is he the only good? Is he what we are looking for? Is he *worth* putting aside all other things, and devoting our full attention and efforts toward seeking him? The Bible's answer to these and other questions is a resounding ***yes*** – we have the testimony of witnesses who assure us that everything that we've heard about God is all true.

Your love, O LORD, reaches to the heavens, your faithfulness to the skies. Your righteousness is like the mighty mountains, your justice like the great deep. O LORD, you preserve both man and beast. How priceless is your unfailing love! Both high and low among men find refuge in the shadow of your wings. They feast on the abundance of your house; you give them drink from your river of delights. For with you is the fountain of life; in your light we see light. (Psalm 36:5-9)

The Holiness of God

Holy, holy, holy is the LORD Almighty; the whole earth is full of his glory. (Isaiah 6:3)

The Bible uses the word "holy" from Genesis to Revelation. And it's used in respect to God – as in this passage from Isaiah – as well as about man. But there seems to be some confusion about what "holy" really means, and the confusion becomes apparent when we turn our gaze toward God and his holiness. The common definition of holiness doesn't exactly fit when we try to apply it to God, because it's so man-centered.

Not only that, unless we get a good grip on what the holiness of God means, we can't begin to appreciate him for who he is. There is a deep and fundamental truth about God that the word "holy" is attempting to describe. "Holy" describes his very essence, and the reason we are so interested in him.

Righteousness

The typical definition of holiness, unfortunately, starts with man instead of God – and therein lies its weakness. Most people, leaders of the church included, think that holiness is righteousness – and vice versa. Holiness has become a catch-all word for the idea of being pure, being free from sin, walking in righteousness and goodness according to the Law of God.

Actually there is a difference between holiness and righteousness. Righteousness is a "subset" of holiness; holiness includes the idea of righteousness, but it's bigger than just righteousness. But let's start at the beginning.

Righteousness is a legal concept first, because that's where Jesus starts with us. The first thing we have to understand, in the process of salvation, is that we are sinners. And sin is defined *only* in God's Law – that's the measure that God uses to determine whether we are acceptable to him. Sin is, to be specific, a refusal to do what God told us to do in his Law. He is the King, and we have rebelled against him.

The reason this is so bad is because God requires perfection from all of his works. Not only did he make the universe to his exacting specifications, he also made man perfect – righteous – able to follow God's instructions exactly. His assignment for man was to maintain and direct God's perfect world, according to God's perfect plan. Man is the "executor" of God's will on earth; he makes sure it gets carried out to the letter. But what happens when the executor himself goes bad? The world is ruined, of course, and God's will is not carried out. God's blessings turn into curses. That can only mean war, between God and man and between man and man.

For example, perhaps you've seen a plumb line at work. It's a tool that construction workers use when they are building a wall. It consists of a brass "bob" on the end of a string. The worker holds it up against the wall that he's building to see if the wall is straight and true, or whether it's crooked. This is important because a crooked wall can't hold the weight of the building and roof; it will collapse, even if it's just a little bit off.

In the same way, God uses his Law as a "plumb line" on our lives. All he has to do is hold it up against us to see if we are crooked – which is another word for "sinful." If we aren't living our lives exactly as the Law of God requires, if we aren't doing exactly what he told us to do in his Creation, then we are *not righteous*. We are rebellious. It's an easy process, this requirement of checking ourselves with the Law of God; and it's crucial to our success. Because if we are the least bit off from the "righteous requirements of the Law," then we can't possibly please God. "And if we are careful to obey *all* this Law before the LORD our God, as he has commanded us, *that* will be our righteousness." (Deuteronomy 6:25)

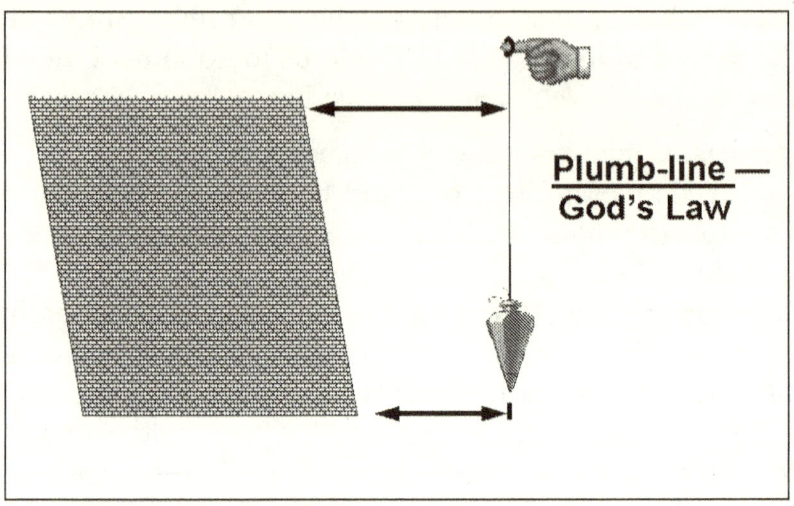

Figure 1 – Righteousness: straight with God's Law?

Nor could we survive in Heaven without perfect righteousness. We would fail God again there, and collapse under the weight of God's eternal glory. He can't use us in this world or the next, if we're the least bit off from the Law.

If it were just a matter of adjusting to some laws, the situation wouldn't be as bad as it is. The deeper problem is the *attitude* we have toward God. In our heart of hearts, we don't want God around. We don't want him interfering with our lives. We certainly don't want him ruling over us; we want to rule ourselves. And we don't like him; we don't like his ways or values or righteous character. We are rebellious and hard-hearted toward God, and we are determined not to reconcile on his terms.

We can better appreciate how broken we are when we find out that obedience to God actually only comes out of a heart that is enamored with God, and finds its sole delight in God and in doing his will. Someone who loves God will love to do his will. And that is our worst characteristic: we have, as sinners, an innate hatred for God now. We prefer pleasures from other sources; we have found replacements for God in our hearts. So, we can't help but be broken, perverse sinners. We are like clay pots designed to hold God in our hearts, but now we're lying shattered and useless in the dirt.

The Gospel is the good news that Jesus can make us righteous – or straight – according to the Law's demands, and bring us back to God. All we have to do is turn to him for help. He simply steps in between us and the Law, and now the Law sees him instead of us. There's no question as to whether Jesus lines up with the Law! He's the only man who fulfills the Law's strict requirements. And he "covers" us with his own righteousness. The Law can't tear us down as worthless; Jesus protects us from God's wrath. That's what the Bible means by "justification."

> Therefore, since we have been justified through faith, we have peace with God through our Lord Jesus Christ, through whom we have gained access by faith into this grace in which we now stand. And we rejoice in the hope of the glory of God. (Romans 5:1-2)

But the problem still remains about changing our attitude towards God. So, Jesus pulls us back up, like lifting up a sagging, broken-down wall, so that we lean on him and *become* straight or righteous in our minds and hearts. He enables us to *love God.* The legal standing becomes a real standing in Christ. This is what the Bible means by "sanctification." Notice that we don't stand on our own; we stand "in Christ" the Righteous One. The only reason we love God and do his will is because Christ's Spirit fills us, takes us over, changes us, and forms us into Christ's image. There is the secret to our eternal life with God.

> And we, who with unveiled faces all reflect the Lord's glory, are being transformed into his likeness with ever-increasing glory, which comes from the Lord, who is the Spirit. (2 Corinthians 3:18)

So, righteousness deals with two things: ***first*** we have to be saved or protected from the *consequences* of our sin and our waywardness from God's Law. Remember that the Law demands the death of the sinner! Christ's righteousness saves us from God's wrath by standing over us and protecting us like a shield from the Law's penalties. ***Second***, we have to change and stop our sinning if we hope to see God. He hates sin; he won't allow it into his presence. Again, Christ's righteousness serves us here too, by providing the "scaffolding," if you will, against which our lives are rebuilt into his image. We become like Christ, pure of heart and willing servants to God.

Holiness goes further than this, however. Holiness requires the step of righteousness, and it stands on righteousness as on a foundation; but it reaches up for something even greater than the right to stand before God without penalty. The reason we know this is true is because the word "holy" is applied to God himself.

God is holy

If holiness meant only purity and sinlessness, that would hardly begin to describe God's glory. Of course God is pure! Of course God is righteous! The Law describes God's very nature; he *is* the Law. That's like saying that water is wet.

Let's use an example. Suppose you were making a stone wall, and each stone had to be the correct length. You would use a ruler to measure the stone. We justifiably ask the question "is the stone the right length?" But to ask "is the ruler the right length?" is asking the obvious. Of course it is; that's why we're using it as the standard for the stones.

To ask "is God righteous?" is the same kind of thing. Of course he's righteous – he himself *is* the standard that he uses to judge the rest of us!

But to ask "is God holy?" is to ask an interesting and illuminating question. It goes further into the nature of God than simply whether or not he is righteous.

In order to understand God's holiness, however, we have to come at it in a certain way. This isn't an academic question. God's holiness brings an aura of dread and joy with it; when we approach God, we change – his presence does something to us to make us ready and willing to appreciate who he is. Only those who *want* to see God will appreciate him. And those who see God will *want* him – *only* him. *That's* holiness.

For example, Isaiah the prophet was brought before God's throne and a dread came over him.

> In the year that King Uzziah died, I saw the Lord seated on a throne, high and exalted, and the train of his robe filled the temple. Above him were seraphs, each with six wings: With two wings they covered their faces, with two they covered their feet, and with two they were flying. And they were calling to one another: "Holy, holy, holy is the LORD Almighty; the whole earth is full of his glory." At the sound of their voices the doorposts and thresholds shook and the temple was filled with smoke. "Woe to me!" I cried. "I am ruined! For I am a man of unclean lips, and I live among a people of unclean lips, and my eyes have seen the King, the LORD Almighty." Then one of the seraphs flew to me with a live coal in his hand, which he had taken with tongs from the altar. With it he touched my mouth and said, "See, this has touched your lips; your guilt is taken away and your sin atoned for." (Isaiah 6:1-7)

The holiness of God struck Isaiah; there was something about God that brought the Prophet's attention to a sharp focus on God himself. Never had he seen such purity and righteousness before. Isaiah was being prepared for a certain kind of ministry (see the rest of chapter 6) and he had to see a profound and heart-changing truth in God. God *demands* righteousness and purity, because no impure creature can come before him and live; everything else, even the best of men, are unclean in the light of this God. Men might think that they are righteous, but they don't know what righteousness is until they are standing in front of him. God is the standard by which all of us are judged. Isaiah now appreciated a truth that used to be so academic. He knew about the righteousness of God, but now he *sees* a righteous God who, by contrast, puts our degraded spiritual state in its proper light.

Hearsay and tradition don't teach us the whole truth about God. Even when we read the Bible, the truth about him can wash over us like water on a duck and make no impression on us. Sunday School lessons and sermons can attempt to describe God, but there's something about coming into God's presence that brings the truth to life; the stories become real. He changes us into worshipers.

The primary thing that strikes us about God when we see him is that ***God alone is glorious***. He is self-existent; he is the origin of all things; everything else is created by him, or derived from him, or depends on him, or is a wicked and rebellious force working against him. He alone is God; there is no other god besides him, nor can there be.

> You were shown these things so that you might know that the LORD is God; besides him there is no other. (Deuteronomy 4:35)
>
> Acknowledge and take to heart this day that the LORD is God in heaven above and on the earth below. There is no other. (Deuteronomy 4:39)

God is the only thing there is to live for. If we've known anything of goodness in this world, it all came from the hand of God who alone is pure goodness. Wisdom, power, majesty, judgment, beauty – all these things and more are only truly understood by seeing them in God. All other things that claim these names are poor copies compared to God who is the original of them all. As he described himself, "I AM WHO I AM … This is my Name forever, the Name by which I am to be remembered from generation to generation." (Exodus 3:14-15) God alone can say, "I AM." Everything and everyone else can only say, "I was *created*, I am only a copy of the original in God, I can only exist by God's will, I am designed to lead others back to my God."

There is only one right way to see God – through this concept of his holiness, or uniqueness, or glory. All the rest of creation starts here with God, like the hub of a wheel holding the spokes that radiate out from it. Once we see the true God, all sorts of things get straightened out in our minds and hearts. For example, we know now what **sin** is – it's rejecting *this* God, as if we don't need him. We understand what **righteousness** is – it's doing *this* God's will, because nobody else's laws can bring about such perfection and blessing in our lives. We know now what **holiness** is – living in the presence of *this* God, because only he is the source of pure bliss to the soul; he is all that we need. And we know now why there has to be a **Heaven** and a **Hell** – Heaven for those who want to live with *this* God, and Hell for those who would so insult the glory of God by rejecting him in any way. Only the utterly perverse and spiritually dead and blind would do such an incredibly stupid thing.

> For from him and through him and to him are all things. To him be the glory forever! (Romans 11:36)

Struck with the holiness of God

Something is wrong with today's Christianity. The "knowledge of God" doesn't seem to be changing many people.

Some come at it as if it's an academic exercise: they learn doctrine *about* God, they memorize Scripture, they go to church and "worship" God – but their worship doesn't change their hearts and lives. They are much more interested in their own activities in church, in how they feel and what they think, than they are in meeting God face to face. They love the singing and music, they love the church functions, they love the "fellowship" with each other – but that's pretty much the extent of their church life. It doesn't go any deeper than a social get-together with other Christians – in today's church jargon, a "celebration."

But if you truly come into God's presence, which is the whole point of worship, some fundamental things happen to you. We know what these things are by the experiences that the saints in Bible times had. We can't take our modern culture as the norm here; few find God in our day. The Bible saints, however, are on record for having seen and experienced God – and their encounters with him were startling. Take, for example, the experience that the Israelites had when they finished building the Temple in Jerusalem.

> When Solomon finished praying, fire came down from Heaven and consumed the burnt offering and the sacrifices, and the glory of the LORD filled the temple. The priests could not enter the temple of the LORD because the glory of the LORD filled it. When all the Israelites saw the fire coming down and the glory of the LORD above the temple, they knelt on the pavement with their faces to the ground, and they worshiped and gave thanks to the LORD, saying, "He is good; his love endures forever." (2 Chronicles 7:1-3)

You might argue that this was an extraordinary event; such things don't usually happen in worship services, nor should we expect them to happen (at least the way we worship!). But that's precisely my point: when God actually showed up, the extraordinary happened. And if you were transported from your humdrum, routine church service into the halls of Heaven, you would experience something you would never forget for the rest of your life. It's just too easy to sit back comfortably in our churches and be satisfied with a "business-as-usual" approach to worship. But when you actually touch God (instead of just hearing about him in a sermon) you will be shocked and amazed over the only God, a God who is like no other. He forces his way into your life with an overwhelming reality that you won't find anywhere else in this world.

Nothing else is like God

Our lives here in this world are confusing us. We think that life is good, we think that man is wise, we think that nations are powerful – but actually we've satisfied ourselves with shadows and shallowness. Solomon was right: there is nothing but emptiness and meaninglessness in this world, in this creation under the sun. The real world is God's, not our empty one.

> I have seen all the things that are done under the sun; all of them are meaningless, a chasing after the wind. (Ecclesiastes 1:14)

We think that our possessions are worth something, when really they are quite unable to give us true joy. We think that we have friends, but they only last during good times and then loneliness returns. We think that family is dependable, but in times of trouble they can turn into enemies. Just when we surround ourselves with the "good" things of this world, something happens and they take wing and fly away, leaving us destitute and empty.

Jesus taught us this once when the rich young ruler came to him and called him "good teacher." (Luke 18:18) *No*, Jesus corrected him. Nobody, and nothing, is *good* except God alone.

You have a dim idea of what goodness is because you heard and saw a few things that appealed to you. But you haven't seen real goodness until you get a clear view of God himself, the source of all these things that we enjoy.

When we live for the "good" things in this world, it's as if we have settled for mud puddles of water when we could have far better. Why not trace that water to its source? Why not look for the spring that feeds the rivers, the fresh, ever-flowing water instead of the stagnant ponds? Why not look for the God who made the world, instead of being satisfied with the limitations of this world that prove empty all too often?

You have probably heard the fable of the goose that laid the golden egg. Most people would love to have a few of those golden eggs! But the wise ones will look for the goose itself, and then they can have all the eggs they want.

God made this world to please us and bless us, but it was never intended to replace God in our hearts. We were supposed to have the wisdom and desire to seek the Creator instead of settling down with just his creation. Particularly now we need to seek him, since we've "muddied the waters" and turned God's perfect creation into a broken, murderous, perverted carnival of wickedness that is only fit to be destroyed. Unfortunately the world is full of fools who are going to ruin themselves trying to squeeze the last drop of enjoyment from this dirty world. They are all going to die unfulfilled.

There are a few, however, who have seen how futile it is to live for this world, and they have turned their hearts and minds toward God to find what they need in him. They know that the source is much better than the puddle. This attitude is in itself *holiness*: they don't want this world; they want *God*.

> Whom have I in Heaven but you? And earth has nothing I desire besides you. My flesh and my heart may

> fail, but God is the strength of my heart and my portion forever. (Psalm 73:25-26)

What do they find in God? That God is perfect, and amazing, and unique, in every aspect. Nobody else and nothing else compares to what we find in God. Creation reflects his glory in many ways, but it is only a reflection. It's like comparing a candle with the sun: both give light, but the sun is overpowering in comparison with the candle. For example, man has wisdom and strength, but these are only a reflection of God's power and wisdom. If you want to see the source of all wisdom, the very definition of wisdom, the true glory of wisdom, you don't turn to man. You will see these things in their essence and glory only in God.

Unique in every way

A good place to start if you want to know God is to list his attributes, or characteristics. And another list you can make are all the names of God in the Bible. These are concrete realities that describe who God is, and what he does. The delight of the saints is to turn to each of these attributes and names and explore the depth of how God truly is what these names describe. Nothing else compares with him; everything else in creation is a disappointing, pale reflection of the reality of the thing in God.

For example, let's take the idea of wisdom. When we look at God's wisdom, we will immediately realize that his wisdom is different from all other "wisdom" in creation. It is unique with him.

- God is the **source** of wisdom – all other wisdom comes from God's wisdom, and is wise only when it reflects what he thinks. Man's wisdom only works when it comes from God's wisdom. We have to sit at his feet first if we want to learn anything about truth.

- God's wisdom is the **best** – when everyone else has spoken, we still only have limited viewpoints and many blind spots. Not so when God speaks. He knows completely, and his wisdom fills in our blanks and guides us unerringly where we can't see. You can use this wisdom to build your life on solid rock; there are no weak points in his wisdom.

- God is the very **definition** of wisdom – we know what wisdom is only by studying his wisdom. God's wisdom is the very foundation of Creation, the design and purpose behind all things. Only God's wisdom shows us the way the world is designed to work, and the direction we need to take to serve him and build his Kingdom. Our wisdom only works when it follows God's original pattern.

- God is the **foundation** of all wisdom – man's wisdom will only work when it starts with, guides itself by, and ends with God's wisdom. Man's works are wise only when founded in some real way on God's wisdom.

- God's is the **only** wisdom – actually man's wisdom is at best only a copy and a shadow of God's wisdom. We could do without what man thinks, but we can't live without God's wisdom. This saves people; this fixes problems. Man's wisdom can only point back to God in humility, in utter dependence. Without his wisdom we are nothing.

Now it's one thing to know that all this is true about God; it's quite another thing to stand before his wisdom and be crushed with it, to be bowed down before it and be humbled by it and give in to it and desire it. A view of the glory of God's wisdom will take your breath away. To think that you are standing in the presence of the One who made the entire universe with wisdom and understanding – who are we to challenge this wisdom? You will be immediately convinced that, until now, you only thought you knew something. You don't know anything as God does; you never will. Why were you so content to ignore his wisdom for so long? There is no competition with God. Your desire now is to stand on his wisdom, to feed from it, to fear him for his wisdom and carefully walk in its light. In other words, you are getting a glimpse of his ***holiness*** – the fact that *only* God has wisdom, and all else depends on him alone for his wisdom.

In contrast, it's just too easy, even for Christians, to live without God. We will tolerate news about God for an hour or so at church, but life is just too full of interesting and pleasing things that suit us very well. Or, the problems of life are so distressing and overwhelming that we are completely taken up with worries and with plotting our escape from our problems using the world's ways and resources. Either way, we don't go back to God to *learn* and fill our lives with his precious wisdom that we so desperately need. We aren't actively building our lives around *him*. And that is perverse and insulting to "the only wise God" – it's the very opposite of holiness. It's rebellion against God.

Captivated with God

Set us in front of God's throne, however, and the picture completely changes. Man's holiness consists of having this attitude of openness toward God's holiness, his uniqueness, the fact that we need only him. Suddenly our world becomes a shadow, an empty promise, a vague darkness that dissipates in the light of the glory of God. Compared to God, nothing is good or fulfilling. If we have God, we need nothing else. If we don't have God, nothing else will fulfill us or save us. In God's light, we have only one real problem left to solve before we die: how are we going to be allowed to stand in his presence and enjoy him? All other problems become "light and momentary troubles" that are of no more importance to us than a leaf falling to the ground.

> One thing I ask of the LORD, this is what I seek: that I may dwell in the house of the LORD all the days of my life, to gaze upon the beauty of the LORD and to seek him in his temple. (Psalm 27:4)

When we see the glory of God, and are captivated with him alone, and we fear only him and we want to live for him alone, *that's* what holiness means for us.

In the Old Testament Temple, there were vessels and articles that were "consecrated" or made holy. They were not to be used for common purposes; they were only for the service of God in his Temple. The Hebrew word for "holy" means this setting apart for God's use alone. The New Testament works on the same idea.

> To the church of God in Corinth, to those sanctified in Christ Jesus and called to be holy. (1 Corinthians 1:2)

> Therefore, I urge you, brothers, in view of God's mercy, to offer your bodies as living sacrifices, holy and pleasing to God – this is your spiritual act of worship. (Romans 12:1)

> For God, who said, "Let light shine out of darkness," made his light shine in our hearts to give us the light of the knowledge of the glory of God in the face of Christ. But we have this treasure in jars of clay to show that this all-surpassing power is from God and not from us. (2 Corinthians 4:6-7)

> Do you not know that your body is a temple of the Holy Spirit, who is in you, whom you have received

> from God? You are not your own; you were bought at a price. Therefore honor God with your body. (1 Corinthians 6:19-20)

Holiness for us is a frame of mind, a convinced course of action, the inclination of the heart, a ruling principle of life. *We want God.* We have tasted him and found him to be *good*, in a way that nothing else compares. Every new discovery of the nature of God draws us closer to him, makes us depend on him more, gives us more joy, draws forth more praise and worship for who he is. We find our sole delight in the Lord. That's the meaning of holiness.

> I said to the LORD, "You are my Lord; apart from you I have no good thing." (Psalm 16:2)

And for God, holiness is actually the same thing. We think he's special – ***and he agrees!*** He can't deny himself; he knows that he's the only God and the best of everything. He wouldn't give us anything less than himself to enjoy, because there is nothing better than himself. If we had such an attitude about ourselves, we would justifiably call it pride. But with God, his holiness consists in enjoying himself and giving *only* himself to his creatures. Holiness is a focused and complete attention on God alone – with him and with us. [1]

This is the only right and proper way to approach God. Any other way of relating to God would be unthinkable. Who can say that God is not the best, the foundation, the source of all good things? Anybody who would suggest such a thing, after having seen him in his glory, deserves eternal punishment – like the devil and his angels. People who think that God isn't worth their time and effort are ignorant; they are fools. One look at God would immediately cure that nonsense. It's like the difference between hearing about how refreshing water can be, and a man dying of

---

[1] See the *Appendix* for Jonathan Edwards' view of what God's holiness consists of.

thirst laying hands on it. It's academic to the one, and life-giving to the other.

This is why the Scriptures tell us that you must approach God in a certain way – ready to find glory in him alone, ready to set aside all of your vain hopes and sins, ready to fear him and do his will at all costs. Aaron's sons learned this the hard way. Even though God specifically told them how to approach him in a way that would honor him and be acceptable to him, they ignored all the instructions and turned their worship into something that pleased themselves instead. They focused on themselves, not on finding God. They were caught up in the ceremony instead of seeking God in it.

In punishment for treating him so lightly (as if he's not the sole object of worship!), God sent fire down on them and destroyed them, right there in the Sanctuary. The point is that, even in worship, the idea is to set yourself aside and make God the object of your desire.

> Among those who approach me I will show myself holy; in the sight of all the people I will be honored. (Leviticus 10:3)

How do we know God?

Since God considers himself ultimately the only thing worth knowing, it makes sense that he would give his creatures the necessary avenues to him. In other words, there are doors and windows to God that are deliberately built into Creation. We can know God by feeling his hand on us, surrounding us, caring for us, guiding us through his Creation blessings and responsibilities. They are all designed to bring our minds and hearts back to God, our Maker and Provider.

For man, we have this knowledge of God all around us, if we have the eyes to see it. In Psalms we have this testimony.

> The heavens declare the glory of God; the skies proclaim the work of his hands. (Psalm 19:1)

What do we learn about God from his Creation? We learn about his power across the universe, about his wisdom in constructing such a superb and balanced system, about his faithfulness in daily caring for his creatures. We learn enough, in fact, to give him glory – or credit – for what he has done and is doing in our world. We learn enough to depend on him, to trust him, to work with him instead of against him, to fear him, and to serve him. Only this God could make such a world, and we owe him our lives and worship. When God is this real to us, we should be living accordingly. In other words, man was made to *walk with God* his Maker and King.

Paul also confirms the fact that we *can* see (if we had eyes to see!) the glory of God in our physical world.

> For since the creation of the world God's invisible qualities – his eternal power and divine nature – have been clearly seen, being understood from what has been made, so that men are without excuse. (Romans 1:20)

As Paul tells us here, if people don't know the truth about God, it's not his fault – it's their own moral problem. They don't want to know what their senses are capable of telling them. Punishment is based on this perverse rebellion against the necessary and appropriate pursuit of knowing God.

Let's put aside the discussion for now about how we've gotten ourselves into all this trouble. In a word, due to our sin and rebellion, we've lost contact with God, and therefore have no ability to know God in his glory. So, we're living in a world stripped of its blessing and joy. How are we going to solve that problem? To know God is life itself. In what way can we approach God now that will bring us into holiness, God-centeredness, fearing and enjoying him alone? How will we restore that connection with God who alone gives us life?

There are two places to start. ***First*** is the Bible. So many people are confused about the purpose of the Bible, and that's really unfortunate. It's actually very simple: the purpose of the Bible is *to reveal God* to you. True, we have lost contact with God through creation, and the only thing left to natural man in our fallen world is traditions and myths and false religions. We will never know God at that rate. But by God's mercy, we have been given his Word that carefully reveals the true God to us.

This makes the Bible a priceless treasure for us. If knowing God is life, the Book takes us right into God's Temple so that we can know him and live. Without it we have no hope of knowing God. In fact, it's so important to the life of the church that it was made the very foundation of the church.

> Consequently, you are no longer foreigners and aliens, but fellow citizens with God's people and members of God's household, ***built on the foundation of the Apostles and Prophets,*** with Christ Jesus himself as the chief cornerstone. In him the whole building is joined together and rises to become a holy temple in the Lord. (Ephesians 2:19-21)

The "foundation of the Apostles and Prophets" is the Bible – in other words, the Word of God that he gave to us through them. The Bible is not only important to the life of the church now, it will also be the *eternal* foundation of the church. The Heavenly Jerusalem is forever founded on the Truth of God.

> It had a great, high wall with twelve gates, and with twelve angels at the gates. On the gates were written the names of the twelve tribes of Israel ***[Old Testament]*** … The wall of the city had twelve foundations, and on

> them were the names of the twelve Apostles ***[New Testament]*** of the Lamb. (Revelation 21:12, 14)

So, do yourself and your church a favor and start digging into the Bible to learn about your God. Everything you need to know about God is there.

Second, we've been given the Spirit so that we can know God. We will look at this in detail later, but we can say here that the Spirit makes the Book real to us by bringing us into the presence of God when we read it. He always works in conjunction with the Truth, never apart from it.

> Yet a time is coming and has now come when the true worshipers will worship the Father in ***Spirit*** and ***truth***, for they are the kind of worshipers the Father seeks. God is Spirit, and his worshipers must worship in Spirit and in truth. (John 4:23-24)

"Praying in the Spirit" (Ephesians 6:18) consists of this very thing. The Spirit reveals the "things of God" to us as we read of them in the Word. God comes close to us, and opens our eyes to spiritual realities. We see them and want them. It's a real transaction; it's the very heart of living by faith.

> However, as it is written: "No eye has seen, no ear has heard, no mind has conceived what God has prepared for those who love him" – but God has revealed it to us by his Spirit. The Spirit searches all things, even the deep things of God. (1 Corinthians 2:9-10)

By the Spirit we take flight, as it were, spiritually and enter the halls of the Temple in Heaven. We see things there by faith, through the Spirit, that bring the reality of God home to us.

> But you have come to Mount Zion, to the Heavenly Jerusalem, the city of the living God. You have come to thousands upon thousands of angels in joyful assembly, to the church of the firstborn, whose names are written in Heaven. You have come to God, the judge of all men, to the spirits of righteous men made perfect, to Jesus the mediator of a new covenant, and to the sprinkled blood that speaks a better word than the blood of Abel. (Hebrews 12:22-24)

Knowing God changes us

As we've seen, holiness has the idea of a focused attention on God. Only God is glorious, and we agree. Those who don't agree with that will never know God. "Without holiness no one will see the Lord." (Hebrews 12:14) And simply talking *about* God isn't the same thing as knowing him; we have to come into his presence to experience his glory and majesty and uniqueness.

We know from Scripture that people changed when they met God. You have to change, for at least two reasons. *First*, sinners aren't allowed into his presence. They have to be cleansed, because God will not tolerate sin (which is rebellion) in his Kingdom. This is, perhaps, what confuses so many people about the true nature of holiness. They think that the cleansing process *itself* is holiness. Actually it sets the stage for holiness. Only the cleansed and pure are allowed into God's presence to enjoy him. Only the righteous, the sanctified, the "set apart" are brought into God's house to live with him.

> Who may ascend the hill of the LORD? Who may stand in his holy place? He who has clean hands and a pure heart, who does not lift up his soul to an idol or swear by what is false. He will receive blessing from

> the LORD and vindication from God his Savior. (Psalm 24:3-5)

Second, there is no limit to God. He is infinitely good, infinitely wise, infinitely powerful. We will never plumb the depths of God. We will spend eternity learning and enjoying and using the fullness of God. For this reason, we will always be changing – from "glory to glory," as the Gospel of John puts it. There will be no end to our exploring and enjoying God.

Therefore, someone who experiences the reality of God undergoes a change of some kind or another; they do not remain the same. Conversion is the first and biggest change that happens, because when we are converted we move from death to life. Once we were dead in sin and dead to God; next, we are alive to God and able to know him. The change is literally a new birth into God's spiritual world.

> I tell you the truth, no one can see the kingdom of God unless he is born again. (John 3:3)

At this point, all sorts of things are possible for the new Christian. He can read the Bible and it makes sense to him now. He can pray, find God, and be heard of God. He can find brothers and sisters of like faith and find consolation and help there. He can resist the forces of evil that used to destroy him so easily. He can follow the Spirit and be cleansed of the spiritual cancer, the old nature, that is still in him. The bottom line, however, is that he can *know God* – and that's the source of all this new spiritual life that surges within him. God is a new light and power that enables him to walk in holiness and life.

He will have new emotions, now that he's in touch with God. First, he will learn the ***fear*** of God. Proverbs tells us that this is the beginning of wisdom – and for good reason. We have to understand who is in control! When we see the Creator, the King, the Judge – and we truly understand the mess that we've gotten ourselves into with this great God on all of these levels – then we're in the humble frame of mind that we ought to be in, and willing to listen for a change and follow him out of this mess.

> Through love and faithfulness sin is atoned for; through the fear of the LORD a man avoids evil. (Proverbs 16:6)

A person who has seen God has seen his only hope. He now ***trusts*** in this God who can do anything. For example, the disciples were amazed at Jesus when he calmed the storm and waves with just a command. "What kind of man is this? Even the winds and the waves obey him!" (Matthew 8:27) With *this* God holding him up, Peter could walk on water!

A Christian now has ***joy*** in his life, because he has seen God in his glory of goodness and love. Nobody is good like God, and nobody can bless us and give us pleasure as God can. Nobody loves us as God does; he will draw us to himself as a husband draws his wife to himself. The bliss, the enjoyment, the pleasure – forbidden to those who have no right, but an eternity of private joy for those whom God chooses for his Bride. In anticipation of this, we can bear with anything in this world!

> Therefore we do not lose heart. Though outwardly we are wasting away, yet inwardly we are being renewed day by day. For our light and momentary troubles are achieving for us an eternal glory that far outweighs them all. So we fix our eyes not on what is seen, but on what is unseen. For what is seen is temporary, but what is unseen is eternal. (2 Corinthians 4:16-18)

> And I pray that you, being rooted and established in love, may have power, together with all the saints, to grasp how wide and long and high and deep is the love of Christ, and to know this love that surpasses

> knowledge – that you may be filled to the measure of all the fullness of God. (Ephesians 3:17-19)

A believer who has seen God finds this world less interesting to him or her now. We used to be completely occupied with affairs of this world; now we are turning to God more and more, and setting this world aside. In fact, we are growing to ***hate*** this world with its perverted, rebellious, anti-God slant on things. We are, so to speak, packing our bags to leave this world. Why stay here when there's something better for us?

> Do not love the world or anything in the world. If anyone loves the world, the love of the Father is not in him. For everything in the world – the cravings of sinful man, the lust of his eyes and the boasting of what he has and does – comes not from the Father but from the world. The world and its desires pass away, but the man who does the will of God lives forever. (1 John 2:15-17)

All this is to say that a person comes back from having seen God with a changed attitude about things. As Moses came off the mountain changed from meeting God, we are also "glowing" with the light of that encounter. We are spiritually-minded; our hearts are still back there with God. Our "minds and hearts are on things above" now. (Colossians 3:1-2) We meditate on his Word day and night, because in that is our delight. (Psalm 1:2) It's not hard to be holy – set apart for God – when we experience his glory. We *don't want* to come back to earth!

> What is more, I consider everything a loss compared to the surpassing greatness of knowing Christ Jesus my Lord, for whose sake I have lost all things. I consider them rubbish, that I may gain Christ and be found in him, not having a righteousness of my own that comes from the law, but that which is through faith in Christ – the righteousness that comes from God and is by faith. I

> want to know Christ and the power of his resurrection and the fellowship of sharing in his sufferings, becoming like him in his death, and so, somehow, to attain to the resurrection from the dead. (Philippians 3:8-11)

This is God's glory

The word "glory" in Hebrew also means "heavy." That's why gold is often described with the word for "glory" – it's heavy and valuable.

In the same way, God is "heavy" and valuable. *First*, the sheer weight of the reality of God takes one's breath away. It's easy to talk about God, but it's crushing beyond belief to bear his presence. The mountains shake and burn when he touches down on them. (Psalm 97:4-5) The seas writhe and split apart when he walks through them. (Psalm 77:16-19) The priests, remember, couldn't even enter their new Temple when God came down in person to bless it. John, though he was known as Jesus' "beloved disciple," fell at Christ's feet as though he were dead when he saw him in his glory. (Revelation 1:17)

The reality of God shocks us. We have never known wisdom until we hear the Word of God. We have never seen beauty until we see the beauty and excellence and desirability of God in all of his character and ways. We have never felt power until we experience the Power that made the universe, that holds it together, that will destroy it and remake it for eternity. God alone is glorious, the only pure, self-existing reality; everything else that pretends to these characteristics are poor copies compared to him.

The glory of God is that he *is* these things; our glory, when we can manage it, consists in trying to claim the same names by covering ourselves with physical trappings. An earthly king is glorious only because of his throne and crown and councilors;

God is glorious in himself, without these externals. He *is* what the earthly ruler can only dream of being.

The difference between enjoying this world and meeting God is like the difference between sipping at a mud puddle and plunging headlong into an ever-gushing spring. Experiencing God is like nothing else that has ever happened to you. Experiencing God is what everything else in this world has been trying to get you ready for; our souls long for something real, and this world isn't it. It's no wonder that the Bible keeps trying to turn us back to "taste of God" instead of being satisfied with the superficial shadows of this world.

And there is the *second* side of the word "glory": the Word becomes credible. Glory also means, "Who gets the credit?" All these things that we heard about God suddenly become real. He really is what he says he is. For example, we thought we knew what power was – until we came face to face with the power of God. Everything else is a shadow compared to him. He really is worthy of being called the God of All Power. ***He deserves to be worshiped and enjoyed.***

This is why Heaven is portrayed as a continual praise and worship of who God is. The enjoyment of finding and experiencing the truth about God will take up all of our time and energy. Praise and worship consists of the awed, holy pursuit of testifying to God that "truly you *are* what you say you are." The act of worship will be a delight and pleasure to us who have tasted his reality; it will be a service willingly given to the God who fully deserves credit. We will be filled with *him*, and then we will discover the true purpose of our existence.

> You are worthy, our Lord and God, to receive glory and honor and power, for you created all things, and by your will they were created and have their being. (Revelation 4:11)

> In a loud voice they sang: "Worthy is the Lamb, who was slain, to receive power and wealth and wisdom and strength and honor and glory and praise!" Then I heard every creature in Heaven and on earth and under the earth and on the sea, and all that is in them, singing: "To him who sits on the throne and to the Lamb be praise and honor and glory and power, for ever and ever!" The four living creatures said, "Amen," and the elders fell down and worshiped. (Revelation 5:12-14)

Our eternal delight in God, and our testimonials about what he knows is true about himself, is going to be God's delight in living with us in Heaven. *That* is the holiness of God.

Creation Holiness

God made mankind upright, but men have gone in search of many schemes. (Ecclesiastes 7:29)

In the beginning, God made the world with "wisdom and understanding." (Jeremiah 10:12) This means that every part of his world had its place, its role, its purpose in the overall picture. Every part was specially made to make its contribution to the world around it, and to benefit from all the parts around it. Like a watchmaker who crafts each piece to fit into the whole and make a watch that works with precision, God made the world full of unique parts that collectively make a Paradise.

This of course requires profound wisdom. Scientists are only beginning to plumb the depths of creation, both on a microscopic level as well as the cosmic level. The deeper they investigate, the more they learn that this world is unimaginably complex, yet beautifully fitted together. The mind of man can only stand back in awe over such a work of art that God has made.

The Keystone of Creation

Man himself is the pinnacle of this system. God gave him special abilities that he didn't give other parts of his creation – namely, to both understand and manipulate the world around him. Man is the investigator, the tool-maker, the worker. Animals, for example, have little concept of how the universe fits together, nor can they care. Man lies awake at night dreaming of new projects and possibilities in this personal workshop of his.

But you probably see the problem developing here. In order to best take advantage of the possibilities of this world, man *has* to be in touch with the Creator. If we don't know how the thing was designed, we'll break it. If we don't know the purpose that God had for something, we'll use it for the wrong purposes and create a mess.

God gave man the assignment of being his agent, if you will, on earth; a governor in charge of God's creation.

> Then God said, "Let us make man in our image, in our likeness, and let them ***rule*** over the fish of the sea and the birds of the air, over the livestock, over all the earth, and over all the creatures that move along the ground." So God created man in his own image, in the image of God he created him; male and female he created them. God blessed them and said to them, "Be fruitful and increase in number; fill the earth and subdue it. ***Rule*** over the fish of the sea and the birds of the air and over every living creature that moves on the ground." (Genesis 1:26-28)

Man's job was to manage God's world, to make sure that everything followed God's will and continued to fit together and work together. After all, the world is an inert thing without someone's hand guiding and forming it. And things tend to fall apart over time (scientists call this *entropy*), which means that someone has to keep everything tuned up and running smoothly. Like the "keystone" in an arch, man keeps the system together when he remains in his place and does his God-given duty.

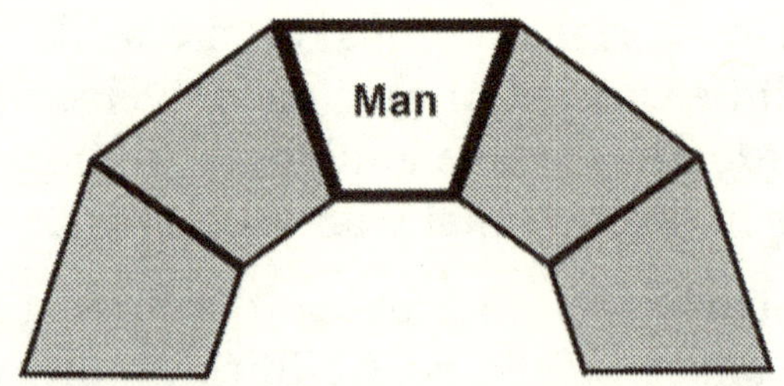

Figure 2 – Man the Keystone to Creation

So, one vital ingredient to man's makeup *had* to be the ability to know God, to communicate with God, to walk before God, to understand the mind and will of God and be able to carry out that will on earth. God ultimately only allows one will on earth – ***his***. Man's duty was to make sure that the world would continue to be what God wants it to be.

To do this *well*, we need to know the mind of God. The reason is that there are many things that we *could* do with this world of ours, but only God's will can bring about a world of peace, health, balance and blessing. There are a lot of options available to man, but only God's will is going to work. All other options will fail in some way.

You can see much ignorance and failure at work in our world today. We have invented innumerable things that we claim will make our world a better place to live, and give us comfort and security. But notice that there's always a down-side to the creations of man. We will explore this more in the next chapter; one example we can appreciate is atomic energy. It's become a fabulous source of energy, and we don't see how we can do without it in our modern world. But the nuclear waste, the expense, the extreme safety measures required, the continual maintenance, the danger of runaway reactions, and exposure to deadly radiation make us wonder if it's really worth the trouble. It's like taking a tiger by the tail. Is the power of the sun really supposed to be here on the surface of our planet? Or have we talked ourselves into believing that we really need that kind of power when actually we don't?

Another serious example of what man has done to the world is warfare. We are able to destroy whole civilizations now. For centuries our weapons have gained more destructive power, easily seen in how Europe was virtually ruined in the last two World Wars. We think war solves problems, and perhaps a war is necessary once in a while – but the price that we pay is lasting and almost unimaginable. Our "solution" kills millions and ruins the lives of millions more, not to say anything about what we do to the environment.

All this is to say that when God designed something to be a hammer, so to speak, he intends for us to use it as a hammer. We *could* use it for something else, but we'll only destroy something in the process. And for as bright as we think we are, we too often won't know what God's intentions are for his creation unless we stay in touch with him and follow his leading. God made the world, he gave it to us, and now we are to follow his instructions in how to use it. The way that God made the world to run is the best plan.

> God saw all that he had made, and it was very good. (Genesis 1:31)

Windows to God

We find it hard to imagine living in close contact with an invisible God, because we've lost that ability that Adam and Eve first had. But they easily stayed in touch with God. He made windows into his spiritual world, and doors to enter in, so that they could and did take advantage of access to him when they needed it.

> The heavens declare the glory of God; the skies proclaim the work of his hands. Day after day they pour forth speech; night after night they display knowledge. There is no speech or language where their voice is not heard. Their voice goes out into all the earth, their words to the ends of the world. (Psalm 19:1-4)

In creation itself – if you can read it – is the truth about God. It shows his wisdom, his power, his faithfulness, his spirituality. It's obvious, for example, that God has designed the world with supply houses, so that all of his creatures can get what they need to survive.

> The eyes of all look to you, and you give them their food at the proper time. You open your hand and satisfy the desires of every living thing. (Psalm 145:15-16)

Not everyone can see the hand of God in creation, however. Paul teaches us this.

> The wrath of God is being revealed from Heaven against all the godlessness and wickedness of men who suppress the truth by their wickedness, since what may be known about God is plain to them, because God has made it plain to them. For since the creation of the world God's invisible qualities – his eternal power and divine nature – have been clearly seen, being understood from what has been made, so that men are without excuse. For although they knew God, they neither glorified him as God nor gave thanks to him, but their thinking became futile and their foolish hearts were darkened. (Romans 1:18-21)

So the windows into God's world are all around us, but we don't seem to know where they are or how to use them. More on that later. Ideally (the way that Adam and Eve were designed in the beginning) we were supposed to be able to touch God, and talk with him, so that we could do our jobs. There are doors in our minds that were designed for bringing us into his presence.

Specially designed to know God

Man is different from the rest of creation in this: he can know God. He has the mind to know him, and the heart to love him, and the will to follow him.

Stones and trees simply do what the Creator designed them to do. Just as it says in Genesis, God commanded a design into their structure and that's precisely what they continue in, come what may. All of the rest of us depend on that static design in nature.

> Then God said, "Let the land produce vegetation: seed-bearing plants and trees on the land that bear fruit with seed in it, according to their various kinds." And it was so. The land produced vegetation: plants bearing seed according to their kinds and trees bearing fruit with seed in it according to their kinds. And God saw that it was good. (Genesis 1:11-12)

Animals have instinct built into them. It's truly awe-inspiring to study the animal world, and see how they "know" exactly what to do in order to survive – from generation to generation, many of them with less of a brain than would fit into one of the letters on this page. God hard-wired their brains and bodies to be able to live (even to change to a certain extent, to accommodate changes in their environment) in this world. And the rest of us depend on that built-in instinct of theirs so that we can survive too.

Man, though he also has some instincts built-in, also has the ability to know God. And that introduces a new concept to the physical world: we know right from wrong. One has to know that when one deals with God, because ***right*** is *doing what God said to do*, and ***wrong*** is *not obeying him*. Animals and plants and stones don't have a choice in the matter; they were designed to do his will automatically. We, however, were given a will. And our conscience – another special aspect of our design – will tell us immediately when we deviate from God's will. Like the nerves in our body that register pain as a message of danger, our conscience will hurt if we disobey God's commands. It's a warning system, telling us of spiritual danger and the possibility of wrecking God's creation.

We are getting into a profound reality here with the will of man. How God can maintain his eternal Kingdom when a man can potentially refuse to obey him is getting into deep waters where we can't swim. Only God can figure this one out. But the fact remains that we were designed with the ability to *want* to obey God – and that, by definition, includes the ability to disobey him if we so desire. And that's the state that Adam and Eve were in.

We love our free will, and we will fight for the right to choose even the bad in order to preserve our freedom. But we weren't designed to choose evil! The ability to turn away from God is certainly there, but it will be no consolation for the poor soul who exercises his "right." We were designed to love God, not the alternative.

Remember that *only God is good.* All of creation was designed to glorify him by the way it was made. We were designed to glorify him by choosing him from our hearts. It's a glorious thing to see the stars and planets lining up according to his wisdom. But it will be an amazing and even more glorious thing to see man willingly turn to enjoy God. We know the delight when someone actually wants to be with us, when someone loves us – that's different from a slave or employee who *has* to do our will out of coercion. In the same way, it's a higher level of glory to God when man loves him and desires him – and that comes from the will. Love comes from a free heart, not coercion.

So we weren't given a will to do wrong, but to turn to God with desire in our hearts for him. The problem, however, is that the will of man can also insult God by turning away from him. The potential for such a glorious act of obedience also has the potential for eternal alienation and misery.

Spiritual restraints

Man was made, as Genesis tells us, "in the image of God." (Genesis 1:27) This means several things, one being that we are spiritual creatures – as God is Spirit too – and capable of appreciating spiritual realities.

But we are also creatures, with the same physical passions and needs as the animals. We get hungry, we reproduce, we get tired, we desire physical pleasures, we avoid pain and danger and hardship. The difference between the animals and us is this: they have instinct guiding them unerringly in God's will for them; we have our spirits. A physical world can't guide a spiritual being; so, we can touch God, who guides us in the right way to go.

Take away that contact with God, and our passions are going to destroy us. Without a proper restraint, those God-given blessings of being a physical creature will turn into curses. There are many people in our world who live without God, and their unrestrained immorality shows it.

> They are darkened in their understanding and separated from the life of God because of the ignorance that is in them due to the hardening of their hearts. Having lost all sensitivity, they have given themselves over to sensuality so as to indulge in every kind of impurity, with a continual lust for more. (Ephesians 4:18-19)

But a man "made in God's image" knows how to enjoy those physical passions in the way that God intended for us. The body isn't sinful; only the unregulated use of it is sinful. Animals have instincts regulating them, and man has the Law of God regulating him. Each honors God in their own way.

So, we were designed to appreciate the spiritual realities that lie underneath and around our world, guiding our decisions. We can see them, and we know why they are important. The spiritual realities that are underneath the surface support our physical lives and guide them in God's ways, to God's purposes.

Figure 3 – Spiritual realities guide our physical lives

In our God-given role as ruler over God's creation, we were given the wisdom to know how to glorify the Creator by means of his creation. Just as a museum curator knows how to arrange, label, and light the specimens to best bring out their unique characteristics, man could understand God's world so well that he could bring out its best side, the order and beauty in God's works, and thus glorify God who made it this way. Notice how Adam named the animals: he could see each animal's particular characteristics and gave it an appropriate name. He was well on his way to appreciating and making the most of God's works.

God deliberately opened the halls of Heaven to man so that man could draw on the precious resources of God the Creator that were made available to him; he could taste them and experience them for himself. His chief delight, then, in this world would have been to bring God to every situation. When any situation demanded a solution, man would bring in the best – the spiritual resources that he had available to him in Heaven.

This of course requires that we fully appreciate how glorious God really is. If we're not convinced that God is the only good, then we will try to introduce other values and resources and powers and "wisdom" than those of God. We will turn to other gods (actually another name for living in ways contrary to God's will) for what we want, instead of relying on the Creator. But if we truly see how good our God is, why would we do that? Why dilute the water with mud when we can have such a pure, thrilling and refreshing resource direct from God? In fact, we would be careful not to introduce anything that isn't from Heaven.

> Such "wisdom" does not come down from Heaven but is earthly, unspiritual, of the devil. For where you have envy and selfish ambition, there you find disorder and every evil practice. But the wisdom that comes from Heaven is first of all pure; then peace-loving, considerate, submissive, full of mercy and good fruit, impartial and sincere. (James 3:15-17)

You can, perhaps, see something shaping up here: a soul that is infatuated with God alone, who is mentally capable of grasping profound truth in God, and who appreciates how perfect and fulfilling the will of God is for the entire universe. The spiritual world of God guides the works of man.

The mind of God

Again, we find it hard to imagine a world full of peace and cooperation because our world is so much the opposite – full of war and conflict and misery and death. How could people live together so perfectly that everyone cooperated with each other, and nobody made war against another? The answer is in the special contact that man had with God.

Adam was created to know God, to walk with him, to communicate with him. God gave Adam the information that Adam would need to carry out his role on earth. He gave Eve what she would need. All the children of Adam (according to the plan) would each be in touch with God and would learn the

Lord's will for them, and understand the particular part of the system that they would be responsible for.

Now perhaps you can see why it would work. God is perfect, and his plan is perfect. He knows "the end from the beginning" (Isaiah 46:10), and he keeps the entire plan in mind while he gives out parts of it to each human being. None of us knows the entire plan (it's too massive!), but then we don't need to know it *as long as we do exactly what he told us to do*. Each of us has a part of the mind of God, the part of the picture that directly pertains to our duties. Put each piece together, and you have a perfect world.

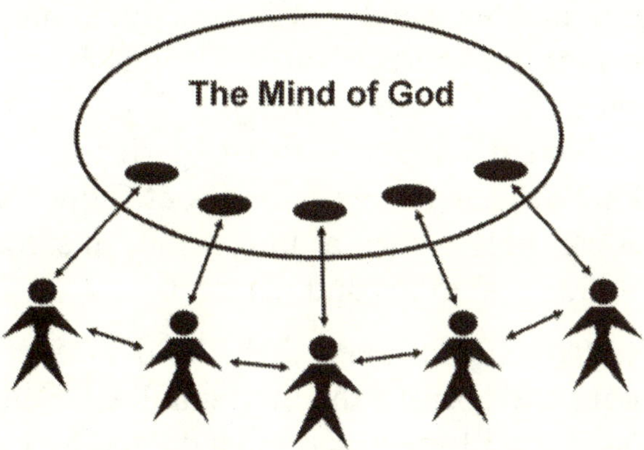

Figure 4 – In touch with God, in harmony with each other

You will also have perfect harmony between the workers. As long as we are careful to do God's will and nothing but his will, we can't help but get along! There will be no reason for conflict if we really love God. We all trust God completely that he knows what he's doing, and that he gave us what we need to do our own particular job. We will never doubt the motives of another person, nor will we disagree or take issue with what he's doing – because we know he's doing only God's will. We all understand how good God is, and we want nothing but God in our world. The system works.

It's like a choreographed dance, or a flock of birds in flight: each of us doing exactly what God made us to do. The animals do it by instinct, and we do it out of our desire for God. The end result is a beautiful example of God's wisdom, blessing, power and purpose on the level of *society* – thousands, millions, billions of human beings living and working in perfect harmony.

Such a thing would thrill the heart and mind of man to see. What a profound wisdom that can organize every detail to perfection, and create a single tapestry of beauty and blessing out of the work of billions of individuals! We can see how God does the same thing on an atomic level, bringing uncounted trillions of atoms together to create a single, fully-functional human being – a reality bigger than its parts. But to bring that many *people* together in concert and peace, willing and able to do their part, and create a universal Kingdom that experiences the hand of a good God (knowing what we do about how obstinate and rebellious man can be!) – such a thing would inspire eternal awe and worship of God's abilities and nature.

So God the Creator designed this world to operate on many levels: the atomic, the cosmic, the individual, the Kingdom. Look at any level and you will see order, balance, the part depending on the whole, the whole depending on the part, one level supporting and yet depending on the next level. The complexity is beyond us, the purpose is also beyond us; but God manages the entire thing to bless his creatures.

> So I commend the enjoyment of life, because nothing is better for a man under the sun than to eat and drink and be glad. Then joy will accompany him in his work all the days of the life God has given him under the sun. When I applied my mind to know wisdom and to observe man's labor on earth – his eyes not seeing sleep day or night – then I saw all that God has done. *No one can comprehend what goes on under the sun.* Despite all his efforts to search it out, man cannot discover its

> meaning. Even if a wise man claims he knows, he cannot really comprehend it. (Ecclesiastes 8:15-17)

But then we weren't made to understand it all. Our desire is to know God, to rely on him alone, to serve him in our limited capacity, and to trust in him to be the King over all. We weren't made to replace him from his throne in Heaven. We were made to enjoy him on several levels, and to follow his leading. The rest is his responsibility. And *that* was the secret to a perfect world – the holiness of God. *Only God is good*. It was our job to make that plain on earth, in concrete ways, each in our own way.

> Holy, holy, holy is the LORD Almighty; the whole earth is full of his glory. (Isaiah 6:3)

Fallen Man

The fool says in his heart, "There is no God." They are corrupt, their deeds are vile; there is no one who does good. The LORD looks down from Heaven on the sons of men to see if there are any who understand, any who seek God. (Psalm 14:1-2)

There are many people who are offended with the Bible's talk about a God of wrath, an angry God, a God who punishes people for their sins. They can't believe that a good God would actually entertain the thought of putting people into Hell. Surely God, if there is a God, would be bigger than that. Surely he can overlook our mistakes and take good intentions for the action.

So, to drive their point home even more, they've changed the message of religion, even of Christianity, to accommodate their new idea of God. They believe only in a God of love, a God who accepts us as we are, a God who will open up his arms to everyone – and that means Buddhist, Muslim, Jew or Christian – who wants to come to him, in whatever way they choose.

I can understand their point to a certain extent. I can't imagine such a punishment as Hell; I wouldn't wish it on my worst enemy. And to think that God would *willingly* put people in Hell is beyond my ability to comprehend.

That is, until I start seeing the depth of man's animosity toward God. Now I know why Hell is necessary.

The holiness of God not only gives us a view of what Heaven will be like, it also puts sin in its true light. If we don't understand God's severe reaction against our sin, it's only because we haven't truly understood what we have done to God. It's one thing to get into an argument with someone; but when they slap you in the face, suddenly the situation turns personal. A personal insult like that isn't solved by more words; it will take bitter humility and a great deal of grace before good feelings are restored again. Before it's over, someone is going to pay.

> Who is it you have insulted and blasphemed? Against whom have you raised your voice and lifted your eyes in pride? Against the Holy One of Israel! (Isaiah 37:23)

God created this world to be a Paradise, and he had every intention of things going very well between him and his chosen governor. But something went badly wrong. We know that because we aren't living in a Paradise anymore! We're in a battlefield, and God himself has taken up arms against the human race. We want to look at what happened here, and try to understand the situation that we're in. Understanding the truth is halfway to solving the problem. The trouble is that most of humanity seems to be in the dark about the spiritual state that they're in and the danger looming over their heads.

Rebellion

Genesis 3 tells us what happened. As usual, the Bible doesn't explain much about the side-issues, like where Satan came from or how long Adam and Eve lived in their innocence. It comes right to the point because it's anxious to tell another story (starting with Genesis 12). First, however, it has to account for our current situation with God. Creation painted a picture of Paradise, but we know very well that our world isn't a Paradise. Something serious happened.

Read the story for yourself, and you will see that it was a deliberate act of rebellion against God's command. He told Adam and Eve *not* to eat of the fruit from the Tree of the

Knowledge of Good and Evil; unfortunately, they did precisely that. And that, the Bible tells us, is the root of sin.

> Everyone who sins breaks the Law; in fact, sin is lawlessness. (1 John 3:4)

But actually there were two fatal events which happened in quick succession: *sin*, and *independence from God.* Let's slow down the action and examine how they came to be.

First, Eve listened to Satan's analysis of God's command. Satan very plainly cast doubt on God's wisdom, when he contradicted the command about eating the fruit. "You will not surely die," he lied. It was a subtle shift, but it was enough to get Eve to think that maybe God's wisdom wasn't what she thought it was. Perhaps God didn't mean to give her and her husband his best; another source – Satan, and the fruit of the Tree – offered her something better. That shift away from God was the critical step away from holiness, or God-centeredness, into a life consumed with pleasing one's senses *apart* from God. This was the sin: rebelling against God the King.

Second, Eve took the fruit and ate it – and suddenly "the eyes of both of them were opened" and they now had the Knowledge of Good and Evil. Satan wasn't lying about this; even God admitted, later in the chapter, that now man had this ability. (Genesis 3:22) The reason this was fatal was that, instead of God deciding for man what was good and not good, man decides *for himself* what is good and not good. Instead of going to God and getting all good things *from him*, depending on God alone to make that decision for him, Adam judges for himself what he needs and wants. The problem is that he uses his own senses and desires as the standards of his judgment! This was the independence from God.

> When the woman saw that the fruit of the tree was good for food and pleasing to the eye, and also desirable

> for gaining wisdom, she took some and ate it. (Genesis 3:6)

Now the entire human race has this inclination to judge things, to select what *they want* instead of relying on God. (The fact that they ate the fruit means that it entered into our human nature; we *all* inherit this trait now.) We all choose what pleases us, and we reject what displeases us. And if we end up disagreeing with someone else's judgment about something, including God's judgment, there's going to be war.

Sin, therefore, was turning away from God. The disaster was that now we will never go back to God for anything, since we're independent agents now. The door was slammed shut on being holy, or God-centered.

This opens up a vital area that we have to understand if we want to cure our problem. *Their act of disobedience led them away from God.* Now they can't have God; they cut themselves off from their only good. They will have death now, not life.

Sin is disobeying God's command; it breaks the close relationship between us and God. It leads us away from God, by taking paths that he told us not to take; and when we wander out there in the world away from God then we're going to find death, not life. This is why (we will see more on this in the next chapter) the Bible lays so much emphasis on righteousness, or walking according to the Law of God, being the way back to God's throne of life.

Catastrophe

Turning away from God, and picking up the character trait of judging for oneself (using one's own senses and reasoning as the standard) what is good or evil, is a toxic combination for life. It brought immediate death for the soul of man, and ultimate death on his physical side.

> Cursed is the ground because of you; through painful toil you will eat of it all the days of your life. It will produce thorns and thistles for you, and you will eat the plants of the field. By the sweat of your brow you will eat your food until you return to the ground, since from it you were taken; for dust you are and to dust you will return. (Genesis 3:17-19)

Now instead of experiencing the blessings of God through creation, man would suffer curses through that same creation. The world was no longer a conduit to God but an obstacle, a barrier that God would use to crush man in punishment. The really fatal aspect of this situation is that man lost his connection with God, and therefore with the goodness of God. Instead of being our source of life, now God is our enemy dealing out death. The result is that people haven't been able to even figure out who God really is, let alone get in touch with him; the doors to Heaven are shut. There have been uncounted philosophies and religions throughout history that haven't done us any good at all for solving our basic spiritual problems; we all die in the end, cursed and lost. No matter how advanced and civilized the world around us may get, we've never been able to cross over that barrier that God set up between us. And separation from God, as we've seen already, is death.

This situation between us and God has even worse repercussions on earth. When nobody is in touch with God, nobody can carry out their responsibilities on earth that God gave us at Creation. So everyone is doing "what is right in their own eyes." And when everyone is using themselves as the standard of what is right and wrong, it's not surprising at all to find everyone arguing with each other since nobody's version of right and wrong is the same as another's. There is war, murder, lust, robbery, adultery, sexual perversions, rage, destruction and much more as millions of independent agents struggle for "their fair share" at the expense of everyone else around them. This chaotic situation naturally happens when we lose touch with God who *alone* is able to 1) decide what is good and right, and 2) orchestrate millions of humans to create a workable world. Without God, we end up fighting both God and man. We will never get along.

Figure 5 – Out of touch with God and man

We can't agree on what the wise course of action should be in anything we do. We can't bring about law and order when everyone disagrees on what the standards should be. We can't make sure that everyone gets what they need to survive when we are so self-centered about our own desires. And even if we manage to put aside our differences for a time and cooperate, it won't be long till the project falls apart again. It's in our nature to look out for "number one" first.

> What causes fights and quarrels among you? Don't they come from your desires that battle within you? You want something but don't get it. You kill and covet, but you cannot have what you want. You quarrel and fight. You do not have, because you do not ask God. When you ask, you do not receive, because you ask with wrong motives, that you may spend what you get on your pleasures. (James 4:1-3)

When man found himself alone, with raging lusts that demanded to be satisfied, and no options for getting back to God and straightening this situation out, he started a new project: to re-create this world to fulfill his lusts and desires. If he can't have God's goodness, then he will create his own. And to this day humanity has been fanatically busy creating a world that gives them the satisfactions and thrills and riches and security that they want. We call it "the good life," or the American Dream, or Utopia. It's a life of wealth and power and lust and entertainment and, in many cases, vengeance and war and repression. We've replaced what God thought was "good" (Genesis 1:31) with what *we* think is good. And God hates it. It's actually idolatry, because we now worship the objects of our lusts instead of the Creator.

> Do not love the world or anything in the world. If anyone loves the world, the love of the Father is not in him. For everything in the world – the cravings of sinful man, the lust of his eyes and the boasting of what he has and does – comes not from the Father but from the world. (1 John 2:15-16)

> Put to death, therefore, whatever belongs to your earthly nature: sexual immorality, impurity, lust, evil desires and greed, which is idolatry. (Colossians 3:5)

Man doesn't have God's wisdom. God can create a universe with parts that fit together perfectly. Man, however, creates a disaster. He can't anticipate what will happen when he creates new machines and chemicals and governments and cultures, no matter what good intentions he may have. Notice that there is always a downside to man's works, for two reasons: *first*, God has a curse on this creation, which means he will make sure that we get hurt and frustrated working with it (see the story of Babel). He certainly isn't going to reward us in our rebellion! And *second*, we don't understand the materials we're working with well enough to avoid potential problems; we're always being surprised by hidden flaws. Just when we thought we found a miracle cure in penicillin, the germs found a way to get around it and become "superbugs." The poison we create to kill insects ends up polluting our neighborhood water sources. Today milk is good for us; tomorrow, the doctors decide that it's bad for us; the next week, it's "good" again. The automobile, a machine that solved so many of our problems of transportation, destroyed local communities and even families as people spread out across the nation.

In other words we have left the goodness of God (remember that he called what *he* made "very good") and are trying desperately to create another "good" out of the ingredients of this world without God's direction. But there's a problem in that: this world wasn't designed to fulfill the heart and life of man; only God can do that. So, as the wise man taught us, we will struggle to get what we want out of this world, fail, and die in the end anyway, having failed to achieve happiness.

> So I hated life, because the work that is done under the sun was grievous to me. All of it is meaningless, a chasing after the wind. I hated all the things I had toiled for under the sun, because I must leave them to the one who comes after me. And who knows whether he will be a wise man or a fool? Yet he will have control over all the work into which I have poured my effort and skill under the sun. This too is meaningless. So my heart began to despair over all my toilsome labor under the sun. For a man may do his work with wisdom, knowledge and skill, and then he must leave all he owns to someone who has not worked for it. This too is meaningless and a great misfortune. What does a man get for all the toil and anxious striving with which he labors under the sun? All his days his work is pain and

> grief; even at night his mind does not rest. This too is meaningless. (Ecclesiastes 2:17-23)
>
> This too is a grievous evil: As a man comes, so he departs, and what does he gain, since he toils for the wind? All his days he eats in darkness, with great frustration, affliction and anger. (Ecclesiastes 5:16-17)

Not only have we cut ourselves off from our only good and replaced it with emptiness, we've settled for a lifestyle below the animals. We're following a progression from life to death; it's a deadly recipe for the "good life" that will only result in disaster. We turn our backs on God, and look for something else to fill our lives with. And since nothing will keep us alive like God can, our souls dry up in lawlessness and helplessness. As a result, man's character goes from bad to worse; and our relationships with each other turn into a putrid mass of reprobation, selfishness, materialism, and general, all-around nastiness. Paul, for example, describes a world without God.

> Furthermore, since they did not think it worthwhile to retain the knowledge of God, he gave them over to a depraved mind, to do what ought not to be done. They have become filled with every kind of wickedness, evil, greed and depravity. They are full of envy, murder, strife, deceit and malice. They are gossips, slanderers, God-haters, insolent, arrogant and boastful; they invent ways of doing evil; they disobey their parents; they are senseless, faithless, heartless, ruthless. Although they know God's righteous decree that those who do such things deserve death, they not only continue to do these very things but also approve of those who practice them. (Romans 1:28-32)

This is *not* the world that God created! This is the world that rebellious man created. And our answers and solutions to these kinds of problems have proved powerless, no matter how much law and coercion and reasoning we've tried to apply to them. God dropped us down into an inescapable prison where our wicked and perverse natures are destroying us, and we have no hope of getting out of this situation on our own.

Independence from God

This all came about, remember, from our deciding that God was not worth seeking out. We didn't want God; we wanted something other than God. Our lives now are in complete independence from God. The norm in our world is to treat God as if he's a fringe idea, a "help" only when we get into some kind of trouble that we can't get ourselves out of. God is only for those "religious fanatics" who need a "crutch" because they can't take care of themselves. The average person is too busy working and enjoying life and creating his own little nest to bother taking God seriously. Life *without God* is normal to us.

This isn't to say that many people totally ignore God. Many still go to church (let's deal with "Christians" at this point; pagan religions have their own special problem!) and "worship God." But that usually consists of thinking *about* God, and talking *about* God, without actually meeting with God himself. Listening to a sermon, and singing a hymn, is not the same as coming into God's presence and touching *him*.

This is a profound and shocking insult to God who alone is glorious. When we're looking for wisdom, we don't turn to God and his Word. When we need power, we look to some other power than God. When we need solutions to the disaster that sin is creating among us, we make up our own rules and try to fix it our own way instead of following God's directions out of the mess. In short, we don't think that God is the only good for us; in fact, we don't even consider him an option.

This is in spite of the fact that God is the Creator and can do anything! He still raises up nations and tears others down. He keeps the planet running, he feeds all of us every day, he directs our steps even when we can't see him, he forbears punishing us with the hope that we will listen to him and change. Even though he's doing all of this and more on a daily basis, we give him no credit at all for knowing what he's doing. We refuse to include him in our plans.

It's an insult to God to be shoved aside like this. Is there any other god or power or wisdom that is better than Israel's God?

> Who among the gods is like you, O LORD? Who is like you – majestic in holiness, awesome in glory, working wonders? (Exodus 15:11)

Are we insane, that we have burned our bridges with God like this and are determined to live without him, come what may? Don't we realize that cutting ourselves off from him like this will be just as fatal as cutting off our own heads? It's moral and physical suicide.

To God, this shows a deep-seated hatred toward him in the heart of man. You may have your own reasons for not liking God, but you have no justification for avoiding him. Independence from God in any way is an act of treason, a declaration of war, a proclamation that you have found this God wanting. He doesn't give you what you want, and so you're looking elsewhere for your joy and purpose in life. In other words, the ruler of God's creation has declared independence and is leading a revolution against God's rule over him. God can't allow such a situation to go unanswered; there's too much at stake.

A wayward wife

Before we leave this, let's go back to the church, lest shallow "Christians" deceive themselves into thinking that they've fixed this deep-seated independence from God with a childish "I believe in Jesus" formula.

We have the command from the Law to love God; Jesus "reissued" that command and brought it to the forefront. He made it a requirement for all those who wanted to be part of his Kingdom.

> One of the teachers of the Law came and heard them debating. Noticing that Jesus had given them a good answer, he asked him, "Of all the commandments, which is the most important?"
>
> "The most important one," answered Jesus, "is this: 'Hear, O Israel, the Lord our God, the Lord is one. Love the Lord your God with all your heart and with all your soul and with all your mind and with all your strength.'" (Mark 12:28-30)

The purpose of our conversion was to focus our minds and hearts back on God. The love for him will come as we wean our hearts from the world and spend time with him. The idea was to fall in love with him, to find in him our chief delight.

Instead, we've gotten rather bored with God. It was fun at the beginning, but he keeps bothering us about *his* agenda (sin, righteousness, living in the Spirit, fighting our enemies, leaving this world) and he doesn't seem to show much interest in what *we* want (to go back to the world!). So, after our marriage, we spend most of our time roaming the streets looking for other lovers instead of staying at home with our husband.

> "She decked herself with rings and jewelry, and went after her lovers, but me she forgot," declares the LORD. (Hosea 2:13)

> But you trusted in your beauty and used your fame to become a prostitute. You lavished your favors on

> anyone who passed by and your beauty became his. You took some of your garments to make gaudy high places, where you carried on your prostitution. Such things should not happen, nor should they ever occur. You also took the fine jewelry I gave you, the jewelry made of my gold and silver, and you made for yourself male idols and engaged in prostitution with them. (Ezekiel 16:15-17)

Our sermons are rarely about God, our activities center around our own desires and purposes, our prayers are about ourselves and our wants. And while we hold God at arm's length, expecting him to leave us alone in our pursuits, we fill our lives with entertainment, wealth, power and pride. Essentially we've redefined our relationship with God: we will take his name, but he must do things by our terms now. Otherwise we're going to spend our time with other gods that will let us do what we want. We continue to call ourselves "Christians," but we are *not* centered on Christ.

In other words, we *use* God – we don't love him. We expect sweet things from him while we pursue our lives apart from him. We want to hear loving words from him while we disobey him. We accuse him of not loving us, and we cry like babies, when he doesn't come through and give us what we expect from him right when we want it. We are busy with everything else in life and have no time for him, except an hour or two here and there. We will tolerate him and humor him once in a while when he forces himself into our lives, but we're glad enough to get away from him and get back to our own interests. Monday can't come too soon for a wandering wife with no heart for her husband!

And what is our response when God accuses us of ignoring him like this?

> This is the way of an adulteress: She eats and wipes her mouth and says, 'I've done nothing wrong.' (Proverbs 30:20)

That's *not* what God wants to hear. Nobody loves God as they should; that wouldn't be hard at all for God to prove against any of us. If we want to restore our relationship with him, we must start by confessing our weakness and waywardness ("Lord, help my unbelief!") and then try to make things right in all areas of our lives. To deny the truth and go back to our lives without God, offended with him because he won't cater to our lusts, is only going to make things worse.

We don't like the rules that God has set over us, so we've changed the rules. If you really loved me, we tell God, you would give me what I want. For example, how much of our prayers are begging, demanding, and complaining about what we want from him? And then, in contrast, how much of our time do we spend just loving God for who he is, and submitting to his will even when it runs counter to our own will?

Well, God is not stupid. He won't let the heart rule the head. Obedience comes first, *then* love.

> To obey is better than sacrifice, and to heed is better than the fat of rams. For rebellion is like the sin of divination, and arrogance like the evil of idolatry. (1 Samuel 15:22-23)

He doesn't like this characteristic we have of putting him under judgment, as if he has to humor us in the way we want to go. Instead of giving us what we *want*, he's going to give us what we *need*. Our ways lead to death; he is committed (in his love!) to change our ways and make us follow him instead. But if we insist on being so independent and wayward, he may just pull back from us and let us alone with our other lovers.

> I will sentence you to the punishment of women who commit adultery and who shed blood; I will bring upon you the blood vengeance of my wrath and jealous anger. Then I will hand you over to your lovers, and they will tear down your mounds and destroy your lofty shrines. They will strip you of your clothes and take your fine jewelry and leave you naked and bare. They will bring a mob against you, who will stone you and hack you to pieces with their swords. They will burn down your houses and inflict punishment on you in the sight of many women. I will put a stop to your prostitution, and you will no longer pay your lovers. (Ezekiel 16:38-41)

This is strong language, but a husband ignored is a person whose soul is on fire. He didn't marry his bride just to be ignored! If you don't love God with *all of your heart and mind and soul and strength*, then obviously your heart is somewhere else and you're going to find out by experience what a jealous God is like.

> For I, the LORD your God, am a jealous God, punishing the children for the sin of the fathers to the third and fourth generation of those who hate me, but showing love to a thousand generations of those who love me and keep my commandments. (Exodus 20:5-6)

You don't hate God, you say? Then prove it to him – love him the way he said to.

> If you love me, you will obey what I command. (John 14:15)

God didn't go to all the trouble of bringing us back to him and enjoying him (the pinnacle of bliss and blessing) just to stand by helpless while we snub him and find something else more interesting to do. He's going to punish us by withdrawing himself from our lives and letting us live in misery without him. David, for example, when he sinned so greatly against God and man, was panic-stricken at the possibility.

> Do not cast me from your presence or take your Holy Spirit from me. (Psalm 51:11)

Punishment

The fall of man led us into a situation of truly tragic proportions. People just don't realize the state that we're in. Being dead to God is cutting oneself off from life. A person may "enjoy" himself with riches and leisure and sport and lust, but that's like rubbing a cancer wound with a local anesthetic. The pain of life disappears for a while, but it doesn't cure the fatal sickness underneath the surface. Someday all these "good" things will be gone and we will stand naked and helpless before the Judge of all the earth. Only then will we realize that what we thought was "good" was putting us to sleep and keeping us from pursuing what is good *for eternity*.

God has put a curse on this world to prevent us from finding fulfillment in it.

> Because you listened to your wife and ate from the tree about which I commanded you, "You must not eat of it," cursed is the ground because of you; through painful toil you will eat of it all the days of your life. It will produce thorns and thistles for you, and you will eat the plants of the field. By the sweat of your brow you will eat your food until you return to the ground, since from it you were taken; for dust you are and to dust you will return. (Genesis 3:17-19)

So we have failed crops and droughts, floods and hurricanes, diseases and sickness, accidents and calamities. Nobody is guaranteed safety or wealth or health. Wealth turns us into misers and makes us distrustful of others. Families wage war against each other. The very blessings that God gave us have turned into barbed dangers. What happened? God has withdrawn *himself* from his creation, and now we're trying to get good out of something that is empty in itself.

And the real tragedy is that mankind has lost its connection with God. We can't find him, he doesn't speak to us anymore, we don't even know what he's like. With God hovering over us in the shadows as a threat, and no safe place to run to, that puts fear in our hearts for the unknown. It's the worst kind of fear in a battle, when you can't see your assailant and you don't know which direction he's coming from nor what he will do with you if he catches you. What is Judgment Day going to be like for us?

By cutting ourselves off from God, we've turned away from true wisdom; now we have to make do with an imperfect understanding and gross ignorance. We have turned away from someone who loved us; now we live daily with apathy, loneliness, and outright animosity from others. We have traded the beauty of the countenance of God for makeup and masks and hypocrisy and superficiality. We have renounced the security and faithfulness of God's hand and now rely on the shifting sands of time and chance. Even if we manage to scrape together a few good things in this world, they soon disappear, and we will discover when it's too late that they hurt our spiritual standing on Judgment Day.

And then there's eternity out there waiting for us. Somehow we struggle through the problems of this world and many of us manage to eke out some kind of pleasure and prosperity from a resisting world. But in the end we will all be brought before the Judge. Then God will unleash the full force of his anger against us, for treating him with such insolence and indifference.

> Tie him hand and foot, and throw him outside, into the darkness, where there will be weeping and gnashing of teeth. (Matthew 22:13)

What a miserable end for a creature who was originally destined to enjoy God and live! God withdraws *everything* that would give man any pleasure or relief, all the good things that man spurned. It's incredible, what we've done to ourselves. Once the favored race of the universe, we deliberately turned our backs on the God of life and willingly embraced damnation and destruction, and brought the rest of creation down with us. We deserve God's condemnation.

> Depart from me, you who are cursed, into the eternal fire prepared for the devil and his angels. (Matthew 25:41)

It's no wonder, then, that God has decided to do away with this broken and offensive vessel. Designed for glory, it isn't fit for anything now in God's Temple. Time to clean up the house.

Old Testament Holiness

And how from infancy you have known the holy Scriptures, which are able to make you wise for salvation through faith in Christ Jesus. (2 Timothy 3:15)

The Bible is actually nothing more than the story of God bringing man back to him. We were made to enjoy *him* (Genesis 1-2); we turned away from *him* (Genesis 3); now God embarks on an astonishing project of opening the way back to *him* (Genesis 12) – but this time even closer than mankind was originally designed to come. This is the heart of the Gospel.

Not that the story will have a perfectly happy ending. So that we appreciate just how deep-seated is man's antagonism to God, we will find most people rejecting even this offer of mercy and grace to get the chance to be right with God. This isn't a game; it's war, and most people will fight God to the bitter end. Man would rather die than reconcile. So the work that God does to restore man to his original purity is nothing less than a miracle, changing a heart of stone to a heart of flesh. Very few, relatively speaking, of the human race are going to get fixed. But those few are in for a rich surprise.

The Old Testament is a huge, complex feast of information about God. It helps to get the "big picture" of the Old Testament when we realize that it lays the foundations of Christianity for us. After learning what we were supposed to be (Creation) and what we turned ourselves into (the Fall), we are immediately introduced to the subject of salvation in Christ (the Covenant).

> … The holy Scriptures [*i.e., the Old Testament*], which are able to make you wise for salvation through faith in Christ Jesus. (2 Timothy 3:15)

So that we don't get lost in the forest, we will narrow our focus to the idea of God's holiness and man's return to the throne of God to enjoy *him*. Specifically, we want to look at the *new depths* of God that are now open to us; the *opportunities* that God has given us to approach him; and the *means* that we must take to find him.

A new depth to God

Adam knew God as the Creator, the Provider, the King, and the Judge of his works. The angels know God in these roles also, as they serve their Master day and night. Satan and his hosts know God as a fierce enemy, a God of wrath.

There remained another aspect to God that nobody had tasted yet. It would be enough to worship and praise God for all these characteristics; but as the Bible begins to open God's solution to man's problem of sin and rebellion, we discover another side to God's nature that we never suspected. The solution that God chooses to rescue man is ***love*** – a love that defies human imagination to comprehend.

It appears first in the sacrifice that Abel made to God. And it reappears in Noah's day when God rescued Noah and his family from the destruction he brought on the rest of the world. But the real meat of the Gospel is announced clearly in the Covenant that God made with Abraham. Right away God promises *himself* as the one thing that Abraham needs in his life.

> Do not be afraid, Abram. I am your shield, your very great reward. (Genesis 15:1)

This Covenant with Abraham was actually the Gospel of salvation through Christ.

> The Scripture foresaw that God would justify the Gentiles by faith, and announced the ***Gospel*** in advance to Abraham: "All nations will be blessed through you." (Galatians 3:8)

> Your father Abraham rejoiced at the thought of seeing my day; he saw it and was glad. (John 8:56)

We may think it strange to see the Gospel first announced to Abraham. But study his story and you will find there all the elements of the Gospel that we Christians hold precious. The terms of the Covenant were these:

- God would give Abraham an *Heir* through which the Covenant blessings would be fulfilled for everyone in his family. (Christ)
- God would give Abraham and his descendants a special *land* to live in with him. (The Promised Land – Heaven)
- God would make Abraham's descendants a great *nation* governed by his Law. (The Church)
- God would *bless* the world through Abraham and this Covenant. (Life from the dead)

This Covenant rules the rest of the Old Testament. It defines the very foundation of the relationship that God had with the Jews, the descendants of Abraham. Basically it promises them that God is going to give them an eternal place in his House, a place from which they can know and enjoy him forever, a place so close to God that they will know him as their *Father*. Abraham and his family are about to step into the Holy of Holies, behind the curtain, and see the depths of the *love* of God.

And to guarantee that man can't jeopardize this opportunity in any way, God also takes on the responsibility of making sure that man will do *his* part. Nothing is going to stop this project from its fulfillment, not even man's perverse nature.

So, God proceeds to eliminate the barriers between himself and man to make all of this possible. He is going to bring the renegade home at last.

The ***first*** step is to make clear to man the requirements for coming before God. At Mt. Sinai, God reiterates, strengthens, and supplements his **Law** so that now it encompasses not only the rules set down at Creation, but the additional rules necessary to restore what we broke at Creation. The Law is God's strict requirements for any who wish to come near him. God will never relax his standards; even though we've broken his Law, the solution is never to waive the requirements of the Law! No, we're going to have the salt of the Law rubbed into our wounds, so to speak, so that we appreciate what we're up against here. The problem has to be *fully* understood before we can successfully solve it. We have to learn what we did wrong so that we can fix it in God's way.

The ***second*** step, obviously, is to change us so that we become righteous. And this happens in two stages: *first*, God removes the threat of destruction of sinners by having something else die in our place. This is the system of **sacrifice** that the Law introduced. By having an animal die instead of man, man is free from the penalty of the Law. Nothing else could be done for us until that threat was removed. "Without the shedding of blood there is no forgiveness." (Hebrews 8:22)

The *second* stage is to actually walk in the paths of righteousness. It's one thing to be set free, but God doesn't want us to return to our sins! The Israelites were supposed to obey this Law now, to the letter. In that way they would be allowed to come before God and worship him.

> And if we are careful to obey *all* this Law before the LORD our God, as he has commanded us, *that* will be our righteousness. (Deuteronomy 6:25)

With these two issues taken care of, the Temple doors open before man and he is allowed to enter in and see God. Leviticus may be a boring book to you, but actually it's the precious and exciting account of getting cleansed so that we can enter into God's house and "behold him in his glory." There we read of the strict requirements so that we can enter his house, but we also see the goal of our hearts: to live with God, and he with us. This is the bliss that man was created for.

And what will man see when he enters the Temple of God?

> The LORD, the LORD, the compassionate and gracious God, slow to anger, abounding in love and faithfulness, maintaining love to thousands, and forgiving wickedness, rebellion and sin. Yet he does not leave the guilty unpunished; he punishes the children and their children for the sin of the fathers to the third and fourth generation. (Exodus 34:6-7)

> Praise awaits you, O God, in Zion; to you our vows will be fulfilled. O you who hear prayer, to you all men will come. When we were overwhelmed by sins, you forgave our transgressions. Blessed are those you choose and bring near to live in your courts! We are filled with the good things of your house, of your holy temple. You answer us with awesome deeds of righteousness, O God our Savior, the hope of all the ends of the earth and of the farthest seas. (Psalm 65:1-5)

> My heart is steadfast, O God; I will sing and make music with all my soul. Awake, harp and lyre! I will awaken the dawn. I will praise you, O LORD, among the nations; I will sing of you among the peoples. For

> great is your love, higher than the heavens; your faithfulness reaches to the skies. Be exalted, O God, above the heavens, and let your glory be over all the earth. Save us and help us with your right hand, that those you love may be delivered. (Psalm 108:1-6)

We read about the God who delivered Israel from slavery, who gave Israel a rich Promised Land, who protected Israel from her enemies, who disciplined her to correct her wayward heart, who loved her as a husband loves his wife. We see the faithfulness of God toward those who trust in him, the God who forgives sinners and forgets their sin, the God who purifies those who come to him. The entire Old Testament is a revelation of God doing things for sinners that we wouldn't have expected, things that are called "grace" because we don't deserve any of it. Out of his deep love for his people, he rescues them and brings them into his presence to experience his fullness as Husband and Redeemer.

The Old Testament is full of the revelation of God. For example, sometime you should do a study on the Names of God. The names of Israel's God abound throughout the Bible. I have a list of over 120 entries of just Christ's names. God's names describe him and his works. Many of those names describe the works of deliverance and blessing that he gave the Israelites, his special people on earth. Through their history, they learned what God can and will do for sinners.

The God of Abraham, Isaac and Jacob – These are the Patriarchs; they first learned the basics of the Gospel, or Covenant, in the ways that God blessed their lives.

The Fear of Isaac – No doubt Isaac learned something new about a God who required his death at the hands of Abraham!

The Lord our Righteousness – God will himself become our righteousness and cover over our sinful hearts to protect us from the penalty of his own Law.

The LORD – God's special name (Hebrew, יהוה or *Yahweh*) that he wanted his people to know first-hand: a God who forgives sinners who don't deserve such mercy and grace.

These realities about God provide much material for learning about and praising him, as we see the Psalmist doing in his worship.

> The LORD is my **rock**, my **fortress** and my **deliverer**; my God is my **rock**, in whom I take **refuge**. He is my **shield** and the **horn** of my salvation, my **stronghold**. (Psalm 18:2)

The works of the Lord are also specially designed to teach us about God. God does things that nobody else can do. In fact, his works distinguish him from everyone else; we can tell when *he's* at work because things happen that nobody else can claim to have done.

> Give thanks to the LORD, call on his Name; make known among the nations what he has done. Sing to him, sing praise to him; tell of all his wonderful acts. Glory in his holy Name; let the hearts of those who seek the LORD rejoice. Look to the LORD and his strength; seek his face always. Remember the wonders he has done, his miracles, and the judgments he pronounced, O descendants of Abraham his servant, O sons of Jacob, his chosen ones. He is the LORD our God; his judgments are in all the earth. He remembers his covenant forever, the word he commanded, for a thousand generations, the covenant he made with

> Abraham, the oath he swore to Isaac. He confirmed it to Jacob as a decree, to Israel as an everlasting covenant. (Psalm 105:1-10)

These are just a few of the works of the Lord. As we focus on the kinds of things that God does for his people, it provides food for prayer. We ask for the same things that he did for his saints in times past.

> LORD, I have heard of your fame; I stand in awe of your deeds, O LORD. Renew them in our day, in our time make them known; in wrath remember mercy. (Habakkuk 3:2)

An open door to God

Perhaps we who are 4000 years further on in history can't really appreciate the benefit that was given to the Israelites at the beginning. With the doors to Heaven shut tight, man before Abraham really had no possibility of knowing God, or solving his spiritual problem. God himself saw to that.

> After he drove the man out, he placed on the east side of the Garden of Eden cherubim and a flaming sword flashing back and forth to guard the way to the tree of life. (Genesis 3:24)

But starting with Abraham the doors swung open. His descendants now had three ways into the presence of the true God (while the rest of the world struggled on in ignorance of God).

- ***The Bible*** – God reveals himself in his Word. This is so important to understand. Man can't simply make up whatever he wants to believe about God. God is spiritual, he is mysterious, in fact he's unknowable unless he makes a move toward us first. The created can never understand the Creator unless God makes us able to understand him!

Over time, the Word of God accumulated as a mass of information about the God of Israel. It served not only as a reservoir of truth about God and his works and nature, it also prevented the Israelites from worshiping false gods. *This* God – the God that the Bible describes – is the true God. We are to worship *him*.

- ***The Temple*** – This was God's house on earth. Since we couldn't reach him in Heaven, God accommodated us by setting up his home on earth among his people.

  Of course they had to learn the rules of the household first. The laws about cleansing and sanctification were strict because God can't tolerate the least trace of sin and rebellion in his presence. Once they got past that hurdle, they entered into the Temple with awe and humility. What did they see there? They saw light, they saw food from Heaven, they saw the blood of the sacrifice protecting them, they saw the angels in constant service on God, they saw the throne upon which the King sat, they saw the signs of the Covenant and the Ark of mercy. The Temple, they found out, was the one place they could go to find the real God.

- ***Faith*** – God isn't going to accommodate man but so far. Yes, he put everything within reach of man so that he could understand and use these open doors to God. But behind it all was a warning: this God is *not* physical. He is not of *this* world. Going through the motions with physical aspects of your religion won't necessarily put you in touch with God.

> You shall not make for yourself an idol in the form of anything in heaven above or on the earth beneath or in the waters below. You shall

> not bow down to them or worship them; for I, the LORD your God, am a jealous God. (Exodus 20:4-5)

Even though the physical descendants of Abraham had all these special privileges of knowing and worshiping God, they were guaranteed *only* the physical blessings of the Covenant. But we know – even Abraham knew – that the Covenant runs far deeper than that. There is the spiritual fulfillment of that Covenant that *only those with faith have a right to claim.*

This qualification of faith started with Abraham, of course, who himself was able to see the eternal Covenant in Christ. All the *spiritual* descendants of Abraham (who, by the way, aren't necessarily all the Jews – see Paul's assessment on this in Romans 2:28-29) will enter into the halls of the Temple in Heaven, which is the true fulfillment of the Covenant.

> Therefore, the promise comes by faith, so that it may be by grace and may be guaranteed to all Abraham's offspring – not only to those who are of the Law but also to those who are of the faith of Abraham. He is the father of us all. (Romans 4:16)

So, while the believing Jews entered into the earthly Temple they were also entering into the spiritual Temple of Heaven by faith. They alone saw the point: that God's people want to see *God*, where he lives, in his full glory, not the works of man. Faith enables us to do that.

> All these people were still living by faith when they died. They did not receive the things promised; they only saw them and welcomed them from a distance. And they admitted that

> they were aliens and strangers on earth. People who say such things show that they are looking for a country of their own. If they had been thinking of the country they had left, they would have had opportunity to return. Instead, they were longing for a better country – a Heavenly one. Therefore God is not ashamed to be called their God, for he has prepared a city for them. (Hebrews 11:14-16)

Strict requirements

This sounds too good to be true – the chance to get back to God and enjoy him! This is what we were made for. And God is removing the barriers from his side so that we *can* do this. The entire Old Testament is committed to explaining and making possible the reunion of God and man.

But – there are requirements. There is *not* going to be a repeat of the Garden of Eden fiasco! *There will be no more sin.* From now on, man is going to live in righteousness.

Righteousness is defined by God, and he does it in his Law. We can't accept man's definition of what is "right" and "wrong" because, remember, we all have a little "god" of our own in our heads dictating to us our personal standards by which we judge things. We have to take the functions of applying judgments and standards away from man and give them back to God to whom they rightfully belong. One standard, one Law, one Judge. The system will only work that way.

The Law of Moses (or the first five books of the Bible, also known as the Torah) consists of 613 separate laws (by one count) that God gave Israel. The Ten Commandments that we are so familiar with are actually a summary of all 613 laws in the Torah.

> Therefore, take care to follow the commands, decrees and laws I give you today. If you pay attention to these laws and are careful to follow them, then the LORD your God will keep his covenant of love with you, as he swore to your forefathers. (Deuteronomy 7:11-12)

One thing you must understand is that you aren't free to keep a few of those laws and throw the rest away. God's house is so unimaginably pure that anyone who approaches God must obey *all* the laws, not just a few here and there. As James tells us, if you break just one, you aren't allowed in to see God.

> For whoever keeps the whole Law and yet stumbles at just one point is guilty of breaking all of it. For he who said, "Do not commit adultery," also said, "Do not murder." If you do not commit adultery but do commit murder, you have become a lawbreaker. (James 2:10-11)

Remember that *just one sin* ruined creation. God is not going to put his Heaven at risk by letting in a 99% Christian. We must be *perfect*, Jesus warned us, just as our Father in Heaven is perfect. (Matthew 5:48) Even in the Church, we must never accept any standard less than perfection in God's people.

Thus you will find a complex and at times overwhelming system of purification, sacrifice, blood atonement, offerings and service in the Old Testament. If you don't understand why each of these laws and requirements were necessary, you should at least appreciate how clean God's house is. It takes all that to make us ready to meet this God!

God is not playing games. He's serious about us being righteous. He told the Israelites that he would not hesitate to punish them severely if they took his mercy and grace for granted and lived in sin while enjoying the Covenant blessings.

> If you ever forget the LORD your God and follow other gods and worship and bow down to them, I testify against you today that you will surely be destroyed. Like the nations the LORD destroyed before you, so you will be destroyed for not obeying the LORD your God. (Deuteronomy 8:19-20)

He isn't being unfair here. He laid out a workable system with the Mosaic Law, the Temple, the Covenant promises, the faith of Abraham, and the kingdom of Israel (the story of David teaches us what the King will do to extend and maintain the Kingdom of God). If this doesn't work, it's not God's fault. The responsibility of failure will lie squarely on the shoulders of sinful men who "will not have this King to rule over them."

Keep in mind, then, that there is a requirement for this privilege of coming before God: we are to obey his Law. In other words, the *fear of the Lord* is the first step toward Heaven. Everything hinges on our obedience.

> The LORD is exalted, for he dwells on high; he will fill Zion with justice and righteousness. He will be the sure foundation for your times, a rich store of salvation and wisdom and knowledge; the ***fear of the LORD*** is the key to this treasure. (Isaiah 33:5-6)

The Holy Spirit

If you then, though you are evil, know how to give good gifts to your children, how much more will your Father in Heaven give the Holy Spirit to those who ask him! (Luke 11:13)

Adam was designed to straddle two worlds: the physical and the spiritual. He lost contact with the spiritual world when he turned away from God; since that time, mankind has had only intermittent communications with that world, and undependable at best (misleading and deceiving at worst – there are other spirits besides God out there!) unless God directly revealed himself.

The difficulties that we experience trying to get through life without God's leading ought to make us ready to get back with him. It's no fun working in the dark! Though most people try, a person can't make it without God; it's like unplugging a light bulb. With God is life; apart from him is only darkness, misery, destruction and death. Every generation seems to want to prove this for themselves.

The Old Testament opens up the doors to Heaven again so that we can see the true God. But even there we have two systems running parallel with each other, and that can be a bit confusing. The Israelites learned the truths about God by means of their history, through the physical blessings of the Covenant. But beneath the surface, the faithful were supposed to understand that God is Spirit. One can't represent God with anything on earth. And his earthly home (the Temple), as Solomon once said, can't possibly hold him.

> But will God really dwell on earth with men? The heavens, even the highest heavens, cannot contain you.

> How much less this temple I have built! (2 Chronicles 6:18)

How are we supposed to know and understand a spiritual God that we can't see?

The answer is in what the Holy Spirit does for us. He's been given to us to help us make the transition from physical to spiritual. It is possible, for those who are filled with the Spirit, to know God, even in this physical world.

Physical versus spiritual

One of the most important aspects of the Bible is how the physical and spiritual levels interact with each other in the timeline of God's works.

Figure 6 – The physical – spiritual switch

In the **Old Testament** the *physical* level predominates. We see animal sacrifices in a physical Temple. We see the children of Israel settling down in Canaan. We watch David pulling the tribes together and defeating the Moabites and Philistines. Just about everything we read about is something that we can see, feel, or hear with our physical senses.

God did this for a reason. Since the solution to mankind's problems of sin and death is so complex – and since the ultimate solution is a spiritual one which nobody can see – he started out by teaching us the answer on a level that we could easily grasp. It's amazing how much children can learn if you make your point in the form of stories and pictures.

So to teach us lessons of his spiritual world in terms of which we cannot mistake the meaning, he used stories describing his works in the lives of real people in real places. The point is there for anybody to see; a child can understand the story; and if we read and believe what God is saying, we can be saved.

Some of the important stories of the Bible include the following:

The Creation of the world
Abel's sacrifice
The Flood
The Covenant with Abraham
The Blessing of Jacob
Deliverance through Joseph
The Exodus
The Promised Land
David and Solomon
The Divided Kingdom
Punishment and Exile
Rebuilding the Temple and the walls of Jerusalem

We miss the point, however, if we think that these events (and many others) were merely physical events that happened for the benefit of the Old Testament saints only. The Bible was written for all of us; the whole Church is the recipient of God's letter.

The physical events recorded in the Old Testament describe the same things that happen in God's spiritual world *in all ages*.

Though the physical level predominates in the Old Testament, we can catch a glimpse of the spiritual just behind the physical, right underneath the surface, if we have the eyes to see and ears to hear. Passages like the following show us that God always did consider the physical level to be temporary and not the ultimate point:

> "The multitude of your sacrifices – what are they to me?" says the LORD. "I have more than enough of burnt offerings, of rams and the fat of fattened animals; I have no pleasure in the blood of bulls and lambs and goats." (Isaiah 1:11)

Didn't he tell the Israelites to bring these sacrifices to him at the Temple? Yet here he is claiming that he hates them! The point is that they were hiding behind the animal sacrifice as if that would buy them a reprieve from the condemnation of the Law, and then going right back into their sin. This is not the way to worship God! The sacrifices were designed to teach us how terrible is the effect of sin. We're supposed to stop our sinning. If anything, the sacrifice would point up the need for something more permanent that would change the heart, so that we wouldn't sin anymore. The sacrifices of the Temple were an embarrassing reminder of the weakness of the system. (See Romans 8:3 and Hebrews 10:1-4 on this point.)

Paul also gives us clues that some of the Old Testament saints understood the ultimate goal of a spiritual kingdom.

> A man is not a Jew if he is only one outwardly, nor is circumcision merely outward and physical. No, a man is a Jew if he is one ***inwardly***; and circumcision is circumcision of the ***heart***, by the Spirit, not by the

> written code. Such a man's praise is not from men, but from God. (Romans 2:28-29)

Where did Paul get the idea that circumcision of the heart was the real point of that Old Testament physical ceremony? Right out of the Law itself!

> The LORD your God will ***circumcise your hearts and the hearts of your descendants***, so that you may love him with all your heart and with all your soul, and live. (Deuteronomy 30:6)

It was always understood, by those who had the faith of Abraham, that the physical symbols were lessons pointing to the spiritual realities in God's Kingdom.

In the **New Testament**, the *spiritual* level predominates. The situation flip-flops, so to speak. Now instead of a physical Temple, we learn of the Temple in Heaven that we must come to. Now instead of a physical land of Canaan to inherit, we inherit Heaven. David sitting on his throne in Jerusalem turns into the Son of David sitting on his throne beside the Father. The Philistines aren't a problem to us anymore, but our sins and the "spiritual forces of darkness" certainly are.

Of course the situation in the Old Testament was also spiritual, but they were required to learn and work things out through the physical means that God gave them. Only by faith would they realize that a more permanent solution from Heaven would eventually come to light on earth. Now, however, the veil has been taken away, the time has come; the eternal solution has been revealed to us.

> These were all commended for their faith, yet none of them received what had been promised. God had planned something better for us so that ***only together***

> ***with us would they be made perfect.*** (Hebrews 11:39-40)

The Gentiles need to learn the lessons of the Old Testament so that they can understand their faith. The Jews need to graduate from their physical system so that they can finally enjoy the spiritual reality of God's salvation. Either way, we don't need the physical anymore. It has served its purpose; the lessons are now recorded in the Old Testament for all to learn. Those lessons are a stepping stone, a primer to something better. Why long for the shadow when you can have the real thing? That's why the Apostles urged us to leave the physical behind and, through faith, reach out for the eternal realities:

> The blood of goats and bulls and the ashes of a heifer sprinkled on those who are ceremonially unclean sanctify them so that they are outwardly clean. How much more, then, will the blood of Christ, who through the eternal Spirit offered himself unblemished to God, cleanse our consciences from acts that lead to death, so that we may serve the living God! (Hebrews 9:13-14)

We do have a few minor physical aspects to our religion, however. We gather together in church buildings, we are baptized with water, we eat bread and drink wine at the communion service, we have preachers and teachers who train us with the Word of God. But we understand (or we're supposed to!) that these can't touch the soul like the Holy Spirit can. The reality isn't in the things we use in our religion; those are "vessels" through which God touches us with the treasures from Heaven. We know now that we can pray anywhere, not just in Jerusalem – because the Spirit lifts us up to the Throne of Heaven.

> Believe me, woman, a time is coming when you will worship the Father neither on this mountain nor in Jerusalem. You Samaritans worship what you do not

> know; we worship what we do know, for salvation is from the Jews. Yet a time is coming and has now come when the true worshipers will worship the Father in spirit and truth, for they are the kind of worshipers the Father seeks. God is spirit, and his worshipers must worship in spirit and in truth. (John 4:21-24)

The list of physical concepts that God used to lead Israel is still important to us, but now on a spiritual level.

Physical	Spiritual
The Creation of the world	***The New Creation***
Abel's sacrifice	***The sacrifice of Christ***
The Flood	***This world will be destroyed***
The Covenant with Abraham	***The Gospel of Christ***
The Blessing of Jacob	***Treasures in Heaven***
Deliverance through Joseph	***Deliverance through Christ***
The Exodus	***Leaving the world behind***
The Promised Land	***Heaven***
David and Solomon	***King Jesus***
The Divided Kingdom	***Division in the Church***
Punishment and Exile	***Discipline of God's people***
Rebuilding the Temple and the walls of Jerusalem	***Rebuilding the Church***

Remember that this is a short list; there are so many lessons to be learned in the Old Testament and they all have spiritual counterparts in Christ's Kingdom. God's Kingdom used to be on earth, among the Jews, and they first learned what it's like to live with this God. Now the Church is living with him, and they too must learn the same lessons. We are all in training for living with a spiritual God that we can't see or touch.

The two functions of the Spirit

Though we may understand the concept of these spiritual realities, living as though they are real will require the work of the Spirit on our minds and hearts. And since God *wants* us to know him, he's not going to let us flounder around helplessly, wondering how we're going to do it. As soon as we become believers, he gives us his Spirit.

> I keep asking that the God of our Lord Jesus Christ, the glorious Father, may give you the Spirit of wisdom and revelation, so that you may know him better. (Ephesians 1:17)

We are about to walk into a strange world, a world that our physical senses won't be able to pick up on. The Spirit will do two things for us so that we can see God's world.

First, the Spirit *reveals* the world of God to us.

> "No eye has seen, no ear has heard, no mind has conceived what God has prepared for those who love him" – but God has revealed it to us by his Spirit … We have not received the spirit of the world but the Spirit who is from God, that we may understand what God has freely given us. (1 Corinthians 2:9-10, 12)

All the saints of the Old Testament who had faith could see God's spiritual world by means of the physical lessons that God gave them. They were lifted up, by the Spirit, out of this world, beyond the physical, into spiritual realities. What they saw there were the eternal treasures in Christ, just as clearly as we see them today. In fact, they witnessed firsthand the realities that we Christians usually only read about in our Bibles. Hebrews assures us of this.

> All these people were still living by faith when they died. They did not receive the things promised; they only saw them and welcomed them from a distance. And they admitted that they were aliens and strangers on earth. People who say such things show that they are looking for a country of their own. If they had been

thinking of the country they had left, they would have had opportunity to return. Instead, they were longing for a better country – a Heavenly one. Therefore God is not ashamed to be called their God, for he has prepared a city for them. (Hebrews 11:13-16)

By faith he left Egypt, not fearing the king's anger; he persevered because he saw him who is invisible. (Hebrews 11:27)

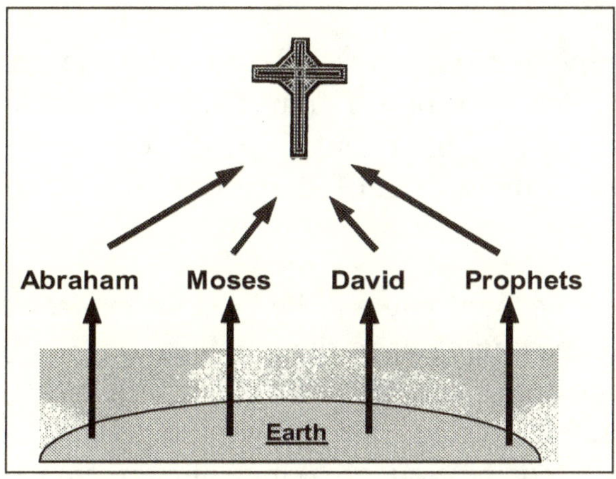

Figure 7 – Faith sees the eternal Christ

Remember that Jesus told us that the Spirit always works in conjunction with the Word. He takes what we read there and ushers us into its reality. He never reveals anything to us that isn't in the Word of God – Old *and* New Testament. The Word reveals God; the Spirit brings us into that same God's presence.

Second, the Spirit *empowers* us to use the things of God's world. The Spirit gives us a new power that helps us do the impossible.

But you will receive power when the Holy Spirit comes on you; and you will be my witnesses in

> Jerusalem, and in all Judea and Samaria, and to the ends of the earth. (Acts 1:8)

By the Spirit we are enabled to "take hold of the promises," to "lay up treasures in Heaven," to boldly enter the Temple in Heaven with confidence to lay our requests before the Father.

> Let us draw near to God with a sincere heart in full assurance of faith, having our hearts sprinkled to cleanse us from a guilty conscience and having our bodies washed with pure water. (Hebrews 10:22)

We not only find ourselves able to enjoy the good things of God, we are filled with power from God to go back to our lives enabled to walk with Christ, and to testify to others by our words and actions about the spiritual foundations that are now under our feet.

> On my account you will be brought before governors and kings as witnesses to them and to the Gentiles. But when they arrest you, do not worry about what to say or how to say it. At that time you will be given what to say, for it will not be you speaking, but the Spirit of your Father speaking through you. (Matthew 10:18-20)

When the Spirit does these two things for us, God becomes real in our lives. Our religion isn't a dry, intellectual, historical pastime, but a life with God. We will experience what Enoch of old experienced.

> Enoch walked with God. (Genesis 5:24)

This is the original calling that Adam had from Creation. Men and nations have wanted to be able to know God, but they always wanted to do it on their own terms: namely, that God would allow them to continue living in sin, while giving them the benefits of Heaven. Under those terms, God keeps himself hidden. Now, however, God is going to restore that original calling and yet keep the proper restraints on sinful man. The Holy Spirit reconnects man with God, but now the Spirit is going to lead man "in all righteousness."

Faith

Faith is not what some people think it is. Many think that faith means hoping that something is true, or wishing for it. "I believe that God wants me to …" Or, "I believe that God is like …" Where they got some of their ideas, I don't know. But they have no Biblical basis for that kind of faith.

Faith is what our father Abraham "discovered" as God was working with him. (Romans 4:1) Faith always starts with the Word of God, because it's a response to God talking to us. Abraham started there.

> The LORD had said to Abram, "Leave your country, your people and your father's household and go to the land I will show you." (Genesis 12:1)

And when God spoke to him, the Spirit of God brought Abraham into the presence of God so that he could see the One speaking and hear these words as from the mouth of God. He had no doubt about what was happening. He knew it wasn't his imagination; somehow God came into his life and made himself known.

So, we have this definition of faith in Hebrews.

> Now faith is being sure of what we hope for and certain of what we do not see. (Hebrews 11:1)

His being "sure" and "certain" came from the Holy Spirit's work of revealing God to him apart from physical means ("what we do not see"). So faith isn't *hoping* that something will happen, it's *knowing* that it will happen, in spite of what your senses are telling you.

Put in another way, *faith is walking in the light of God's world*. The Holy Spirit turns the light on, so to speak, so that we can see the invisible, spiritual world of God.

> I am the light of the world. Whoever follows me will never walk in darkness, but will have the light of life. (John 8:12)

The Spirit of Christ reveals God to us; we see his glory and unique nature, his holiness. He reveals our own hearts and our helplessness and need. He reveals the way to God, through Christ alone. He reveals this world to us and how worthless it is for our spiritual needs. He reveals the treasures of Heaven to live for, the enemy to avoid, and our brothers and sisters in the church. As soon as we are born again into God's Kingdom we start seeing these realities.

Faith, then, is living with those realities. The person who knows what's really going on can avoid danger and take the right road to life. He sees things that others can't see, and the quality of his life proves his confession.

> For you were once darkness, but now you are light in the Lord. Live as children of light (for the fruit of the light consists in all goodness, righteousness and truth) and find out what pleases the Lord. Have nothing to do with the fruitless deeds of darkness, but rather expose them. For it is shameful even to mention what the disobedient do in secret. But everything exposed by the light becomes visible, for it is light that makes everything visible. This is why it is said: "Wake up, O sleeper, rise from the dead, and Christ will shine on you." (Ephesians 5:8-14)

According to the Covenant requirements, all of Abraham's children are going to live by faith, not by sight, because the promises are fulfilled in Heaven, not on earth.

The righteous will live by faith. (Romans 1:17)

We live by faith, not by sight. (2 Corinthians 5:7)

Spiritual gifts

One of the Covenant promises that God made to Abraham was that he would make Abraham and his family into a "great nation." (Genesis 12:2) Abraham soon found out that this meant a world-wide family, across all cultures and races, from his day to the end of the world. The Church shares the family trait of Abraham's faith, and inherits the blessings of the Covenant from their father Abraham.

> I say to you that many will come from the east and the west, and will take their places at the feast with Abraham, Isaac and Jacob in the kingdom of Heaven. (Matthew 8:11)

One of the benefits of being part of the family of God is that we are showered with the blessings of Heaven by means of the spiritual gifts that the Holy Spirit gives each family member. Do you remember the way that God originally designed the human race to work? Each person had a part of the mind of God, knowing enough of the will of God to carry out his or her responsibilities to build and maintain God's Kingdom on earth. Nobody had all wisdom (except God!) and nobody had all the responsibilities on his shoulders. We were all to do our part, and the result would be peace and prosperity.

The Spirit brings us back to that original idea by distributing gifts to each member of the church for the benefit of the whole.

> But to each one of us grace has been given as Christ apportioned it. This is why it says: "When he ascended on high, he led captives in his train and gave gifts to men." … It was he who gave some to be apostles, some to be prophets, some to be evangelists, and some to be pastors and teachers, to prepare God's people for works of service, so that the body of Christ may be built up until we all reach unity in the faith and in the knowledge of the Son of God and become mature, attaining to the whole measure of the fullness of Christ. (Ephesians 4:7-8,11-13)

The gifts of the Spirit enable a person to make God real to another person. Through the ministry of someone's gift, we sense the presence, the truth, the power, the discipline, the love, the guidance, the faithfulness, and the wisdom of God upon us. We are priests working for each other's benefit by bringing our brother's and sister's needs to the throne of grace, and bringing the resources of that throne back to our brother and sister in need.

> You are worthy to take the scroll and to open its seals, because you were slain, and with your blood you purchased men for God from every tribe and language and people and nation. You have made them to be a kingdom and priests to serve our God, and they will reign on the earth. (Revelation 5:9-10)

When we all do our part, and accept the ministry of others as from God, then the church works. Paul breathed a sigh of relief that the Thessalonians saw this truth in his ministry.

> And we also thank God continually because, when you received the word of God, which you heard from us, you accepted it not as the word of men, but as it actually is, the word of God, which is at work in you who believe. (1 Thessalonians 2:13)

Even discipline is from God, and we make a terrible mistake when we don't accept it from the hands of those God sent to deliver it to us. It's meant to correct us in our journey toward Heaven; the wise will see that.

> He who listens to a life-giving rebuke will be at home among the wise. He who ignores discipline despises himself, but whoever heeds correction gains understanding. (Proverbs 15:31-32)

Live by the Spirit

The reason that God gave us his Spirit is so that we can live in his presence. God sets us aside from this world – *sanctifies* us – so that we can prepare to live with him in Heaven. It's going to be an all-day, every-day training process to get us ready.

This is why Paul tells us to "live by the Spirit."

> So I say, live by the Spirit, and you will not gratify the desires of the sinful nature. For the sinful nature desires what is contrary to the Spirit, and the Spirit what is contrary to the sinful nature. They are in conflict with each other, so that you do not do what you want. But if you are led by the Spirit, you are not under Law … Since we live by the Spirit, let us keep in step with the Spirit. (Galatians 5:16-18, 25)

If we do this, then *everything* we do will be in light of Heaven.

> And whatever you do, whether in word or deed, do it all in the name of the Lord Jesus, giving thanks to God the Father through him. (Colossians 3:17)

Why? Because we know that God's way is best. His will is best. His treasures are best. God is the only good, and now is the time to start living as if that's true.

The Spirit is going to work on some critical areas where we need God's help. For example, Paul talks about the great gift that we have in the Spirit, the life-giving power that will change us from sinner to saint. In Romans 8, he lists the kinds of things that will happen to us when we live by the Spirit:

- The righteousness of Christ will get worked into us.
- We will know God's agenda: we will have the mind of God.
- We will have God's life and peace in our hearts.
- The sin that is still in us will be crucified.
- We will please God.
- We will be God's children with right of access to him.
- We will know what to pray for, and we will get our prayers answered.

Without these things we have no hope of Heaven! But by means of the Spirit we can start using Heaven's treasures in this life, so that we get used to living with them. In other words, the Holy Spirit starts building the Kingdom of God on earth in our lives, in answer to our prayers.

> Our Father in Heaven, hallowed be your Name, your kingdom come, your will be done on earth as it is in Heaven. (Matthew 6:9-10)

Holiness in Christ

I am the way and the truth and the life. No one comes to the Father except through me. (John 14:6)

All Christians know that they have been made "one with Christ." Somehow we know that it's important, though we may not be able to explain why.

> And you also were included in Christ when you heard the word of truth, the gospel of your salvation. (Ephesians 1:13)

How this happened, we don't know. It's what Paul elsewhere calls the "mystery" of the Gospel. Through faith, through the work of the Spirit of Christ, we are somehow united with Christ spiritually so that we can now be and do what we couldn't on our own. It's like being in the Ark while the floodwaters destroy the rest of the world; it's a place of safety for us. And in Christ we find the treasures of Heaven that we need to live on spiritually.

The Jews knew nothing of this concept. In the Old Testament they learned about 98% of our Christian faith; the remaining 2% was for the New Testament to reveal. The Jews had so much to learn already that God kept this particular secret from them until the time was right. Besides, Israel first had to get it into their heads that God can't be represented by anything on earth. They were too inclined to make idols and bow down to them! So, first things first – God is Spirit. In their immature state, they would never have understood the idea of God becoming man.

In the New Testament, however, we are ready to graduate to a higher level. We are given the last two important concepts that we need to raise the Jewish religion up from a physical to a spiritual level. But this last 2% is the final step that lifts us up to the throne of God to experience the unimaginable.

Old Testament – New Testament

The Old Testament is not just about the Law. That's a really unfortunate misconception that Christians have had over the centuries. It's too easy to read the Bible superficially and write off the Old Testament as if it has nothing to say to Christians. The claim that many Christians make – that they are "New Testament Christians" – is an abomination. It shows an abysmal ignorance of the Old Testament as well as of the whole Bible.

Paul drives home the point that the Gospel of grace started with Abraham and the Covenant – long before the Law came on the scene.

> We have been saying that Abraham's faith was credited to him as righteousness. Under what circumstances was it credited? Was it after he was circumcised, or before? It was not after, but before! (Romans 4:9-10)

The Covenant is the ruling principle of the Old Testament; it's the only reason that the Jews received any blessings at all from God. The Law was "added" (Galatians 3:19) to the picture because God was determined that the Jews approach him (to take advantage of his blessings) in the Temple in *righteousness*. Nobody is allowed into his presence with sin on their hands. There's nothing wrong with that; in fact, God still has that requirement for us Christians today.

The shortcoming here is that God required the Jews to follow that Law and be righteous – but they couldn't. For one reason or another, they couldn't follow "all" the Law (Deuteronomy 6:25) to God's satisfaction. Not only was the Law severe to the extreme about the least trace of sin and rebellion, their hearts weren't inclined to follow it. They loved their sin; they didn't love God. Even Moses failed God at one point and was denied the privilege of entering the Promised Land.

That's the message of the Old Testament. It's the story of a merciful God allowing his people into his presence *as long as they are righteous.* The burden was on them. There's that richness of God, the holiness of God, right behind the veil, waiting for man to enjoy – but only the righteous are allowed in behind the veil.

The system that God set up to make them righteous was an outward, temporary system to teach them how it all works in Heaven; but it didn't really cure the problem. Time and again the Lord sent prophets to the Israelites to confront them with their sin, that they couldn't keep coming to the Temple in "worship" and expect God to bless them as long as they continued sinning against him.

> These people come near to me with their mouth and honor me with their lips, but their hearts are far from me. Their worship of me is made up only of rules taught by men. (Isaiah 29:13)

So the weak point in the Old Testament story is not the Law, it's the people themselves. They just couldn't keep God's eternal and spiritual standards.

> For if there had been nothing wrong with that first covenant,[2] no place would have been sought for another. But God ***found fault with the people*** and said: "The time is coming, declares the Lord, when I will make a new covenant with the house of Israel and with the house of Judah. It will not be like the covenant I made

[2] The word "covenant" here means an arrangement, a contract, an agreement – not the Law itself. The Israelites were allowed into the Temple to be with God as long as they obeyed the Law. That was the agreement at Mt. Sinai.

> with their forefathers when I took them by the hand to lead them out of Egypt, because they did not remain faithful to my covenant, and I turned away from them, declares the Lord. This is the covenant I will make with the house of Israel after that time, declares the Lord. I will put my laws in their minds and write them on their hearts. I will be their God, and they will be my people." (Hebrews 8:7-10)

Notice the quote there from Jeremiah 31. It has always been in the back of God's mind to provide an alternative to man trying to keep the Law on his own. God has always been merciful toward us. Man is supposed to keep the Law; he was designed to keep the Law. But it's a fact that we sinners are not going to do it. To break the impasse, God must move first.

And *that* is the message of the New Testament. The Son of God has come to apply the wisdom and power of Heaven to the problem. He became a man so that *as a man* he will live the righteous life, as the Law demands. This had never been done before. But God only needed it done once, by his Son, to solve man's problem. Now that righteousness of Christ is available to all who will come for it. It's applied over our hearts (the word "atonement" means "to cover over") so that the Law sees me as a righteous man now. It's a gift, like a coat that I wear.

> These are they who have come out of the great tribulation; they have washed their robes and made them white in the blood of the Lamb. Therefore, they are before the throne of God and serve him day and night in his temple; and he who sits on the throne will spread his tent over them. (Revelation 7:14-15)

It's amazing how completely this solves our problem! We are no longer obligated to keep the Law to get into Heaven. Jesus has done it for us. All we need is his righteousness over us, and in we go with full confidence to the throne of God. Like a key to a door, this new gift gains us entrance to the presence of God.

But this isn't all. The Old Testament taught us that we are going to become *family*; we are descendants of Abraham, and heirs of the Covenant. But how are we going to become children of God? That was never fully explained to us either in the Old Testament. It too, along with the problem of becoming righteous, was left hanging for the New Testament to solve.

The solution for that is the Spirit that Christ gives us upon conversion. We already looked at how important the Spirit is for our walk with God; that we learned from the Old Testament. But what the New Testament teaches us is a new thing that the Spirit is doing for God's people: *he makes us one with Christ, the Son of God.*

> I have been crucified with Christ and I no longer live, but ***Christ lives in me***. The life I live in the body, I live by faith in the Son of God, who loved me and gave himself for me. (Galatians 2:20)

> ... The mystery that has been kept hidden for ages and generations, but is now disclosed to the saints. To them God has chosen to make known among the Gentiles the glorious riches of this mystery, which is ***Christ in you***, the hope of glory. (Colossians 1:26-27)

Union with Christ is the solution of the Old Testament problem. Without relaxing the standards, we are still going to attain perfect righteousness but by another route than the Israelites were required to follow. The Old Testament continually preached the need for us to be holy, to be righteous, to live by the will of God – but it never imagined that God wanted to do something even greater than that and bring us to Heaven to be his children. To make sure we become holy and *stay* that way forever, God's solution is for us to be united with Christ the Holy One, his Son.

We have become part of his very body, his life. Now we can't fail! Now wherever Jesus goes, we go with him; whatever he does, we do with him. He became heir of God's Kingdom and so do we who are united with him. He became the second Adam, the firstborn of a new race destined for the Throne of Heaven.

> His purpose was to create in himself ***one new man*** out of the two [*i.e., Jew and Gentile*], thus making peace, and in this one body to reconcile both of them to God through the cross, by which he put to death their hostility. (Ephesians 2:15-16)

If this is our destiny, how in the world are we going to become one with Christ? It's not going to be an Eastern religion experience where spirits just melt together and become one big spiritual blob. The answer lies in the work of the Holy Spirit. He was always there in the Old Testament, just below the surface of everything that God did with his people. What nobody knew was how integral the Holy Spirit would be to our salvation. There is nothing in the Old Testament that teaches us that the Spirit of Christ is going to enter our spirits and make us one with Christ; this is strictly a New Testament concept. We Christians now know that Jesus lives in us through his Spirit, and we live in him. We are *united* with Christ, the Holy One.

This is indeed a "new creation." There has never been a man in Heaven before. Not only have sinners been barred from access to God, the physical body can't survive there as it is. We have to be changed. Jesus himself became that "new man" to provide, not only a model, but the very mold into which we will all be cast. He is literally our *life*.

> As was the earthly man, so are those who are of the earth; and as is the man from Heaven, so also are those who are of Heaven. And just as we have borne the

> likeness of the earthly man, so shall we bear the likeness of the man from Heaven. (1 Corinthians 15:48-49)

Jesus is a new kind of man, designed to live in Heaven with God. We are to become like him; we will take our places in this new family that God is growing.

> In bringing many sons to glory, it was fitting that God, for whom and through whom everything exists, should make the author of their salvation perfect through suffering. Both the one who makes men holy and those who are made holy are of the same family. So Jesus is not ashamed to call them brothers. He says, "I will declare your name to my brothers; in the presence of the congregation I will sing your praises." And again, "I will put my trust in him." And again he says, "Here am I, and the children God has given me." (Hebrews 2:10-13)

Jesus knows the Father

Jesus told us that "nobody can come to the Father" except through him. This isn't just a requirement; it's also an amazing advantage.

Jesus knows the Father like nobody else knows him. In the Old Testament we learned that God created the world through "wisdom and understanding." (Jeremiah 10:12) In the New Testament we get a name to that wisdom: the **Logos**, the powerful, creative Word of God.

> In the beginning was the Word [*the Greek word is* λογος, *logos*], and the Word was with God, and the Word was God. He was with God in the beginning. Through him all things were made; without him nothing was made that has been made. (John 1:1-3)

In other words, the doors of creation open up into Heaven through Jesus, the keeper of creation.

> For by him all things were created: things in Heaven and on earth, visible and invisible, whether thrones or powers or rulers or authorities; all things were created by him and for him. He is before all things, and in him all things hold together. And he is the head of the body, the church; he is the beginning and the firstborn from among the dead, so that in everything he might have the supremacy. For God was pleased to have all his fullness dwell in him, and through him to reconcile to himself all things, whether things on earth or things in Heaven, by making peace through his blood, shed on the cross. Once you were alienated from God and were enemies in your minds because of your evil behavior. But now he has reconciled you by Christ's physical body through death to present you holy in his sight, without blemish and free from accusation. (Colossians 1:16-22)

He knows exactly what it's going to take to change us, the first creation, into the second creation.

He also knows the mind of God to its depths. He told people this over and over, as justification for what he was doing among them.

> When you have lifted up the Son of Man, then you will know that I am the one I claim to be and that I do nothing on my own but speak just what the Father has taught me. (John 8:28)

> Don't you believe that I am in the Father, and that the Father is in me? The words I say to you are not just my own. Rather, it is the Father, living in me, who is doing his work. Believe me when I say that I am in the

> Father and the Father is in me; or at least believe on the evidence of the miracles themselves. (John 14:10-11)
>
> Righteous Father, though the world does not know you, I know you, and they know that you have sent me. (John 17:25)

This is important to understand because Jesus has an inner knowledge of the Father that nobody else has. It qualifies him for his work among us; it guides him unerringly to build the new Kingdom that the Father requires. Finally, someone knows what he's doing! Now the unsolvable problems that we faced during the Old Testament are going to get solved completely in his hands.

If *we* want to know the Father, then, we have to come through Christ. God has poured himself – his wisdom and power – into Christ, so that *this* road is the way to Heaven.

> For God was pleased to have all his fullness dwell in him, and through him to reconcile to himself all things, whether things on earth or things in Heaven. (Colossians 1:19-20)

But when we take *this* road, through Christ, we're going to see things that we can't see along other roads. Jesus is giving us an advantage here. More on this later.

Right of access

I suppose God could have stopped with giving us the righteousness of Christ if he wanted to; such a gift would have been reason enough for our eternal gratitude and praise. After all, the angels are righteous and therefore get to stand before him and serve him.

But with us God is doing a new thing, something that even the angels "long to look into." (1 Peter 1:12) Christ gives us special rights that neither the angels, nor the other "creatures" in Heaven, dare to claim. For example, God has made us sons through Christ, so that we can call him Father. (Romans 8:15) He adopted us into his family with full family rights, the same rights that Jesus has and the same inheritance that he claims.

In the Old Testament economy, different classes of people had different access rights to God. The Temple was laid out in courtyards, and people knew where their limitations were. The Gentiles were allowed into the courtyard designated for them, but they dared not enter into the Temple area upon pain of death. The Jewish women were allowed in further, the men further yet, and the priests were allowed into the Temple building itself. Only the High Priest was allowed all the way into the Holy of Holies which was the heart of the Temple, the place where God sat on his mercy seat – and then only once a year.

What was happening here? To those who had faith, it was a picture of how holy the house of God is. There are different levels of knowing God. Not everyone has the same access rights, and therefore there are different opportunities of knowing him.

We Christians are called to go to Heaven. God tells us in his Word to start thinking about what it's going to be like to live there.

> Since, then, you have been raised with Christ, set your hearts on things above, where Christ is seated at the right hand of God. Set your minds on things above, not on earthly things. For you died, and your life is now hidden with Christ in God. (Colossians 3:1-3)

So, if there's a Temple in Heaven, do the same rules still hold? What will we find there? Who is allowed into the Temple in Heaven?

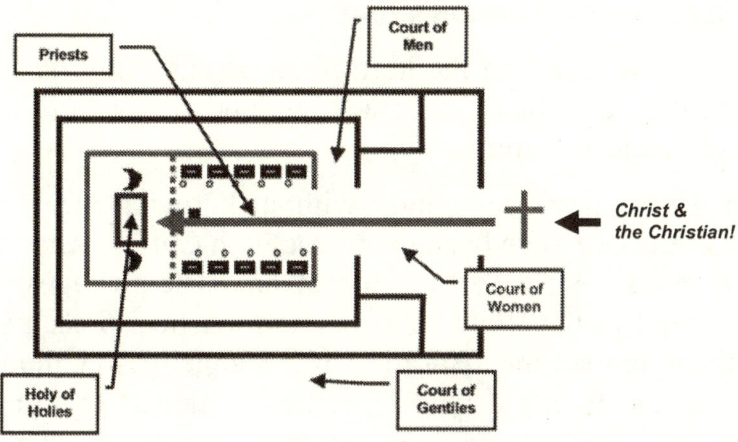

Figure 8 – Into the heart of the Temple!

In the New Testament the rules have changed because *now we are one with Christ.* He has full access rights. While the Jewish people look on in wonder ("Gentiles aren't allowed in there!"), we walk *right in past* them into the Temple area. To the amazement of the priests, we walk up the steps with Jesus into the Temple itself. And over the objections of the high priest, Jesus rips the curtain down and brings us into the presence of God. Union with Christ has erased all the old caste distinctions. [3]

> You are all sons of God through faith in Christ Jesus, for all of you who were baptized into Christ have clothed yourselves with Christ. ***There is neither Jew nor Greek, slave nor free, male nor female, for you are all one in Christ Jesus.*** If you belong to Christ, then you are Abraham's seed, and heirs according to the promise. (Galatians 3:26-29)

> To him who loves us and has freed us from our sins by his blood, and has made us to be a kingdom and ***priests*** to serve his God and Father – to him be glory and power for ever and ever! Amen. (Revelation 1:5-6)

[3] This is, by the way, the outline of the book of Hebrews.

Know God as Jesus knows him

Now we've come to the high point of our study. There's an astonishing reason that God makes us one with Christ and then brings us so close to him.

Christians know (seemingly without knowing *why*!) that it's important that we have been made one with Christ. And they also know that we were called to know God. The passages for both ideas abound in the Bible. Pastors and teachers preach sermons about them all the time. But for some strange reason, though they appreciate the fact that God's people are united to Christ, they stop short at the Temple door and refuse to *go in*. They don't seem to know *why* we are made one with Christ.

Now the time has come to put these two ideas together.

We have been made one with Christ

so that we will know God as <u>Jesus</u> knows him!

This is the most profound and exciting idea in the entire Bible. *Nobody* knows God as Jesus knows him. The angels know him as their Master, the devil knows him as the Judge and God of wrath, creation knows him as its Creator – but only Jesus knows God as the Father. All other creatures are designed with appropriate limitations; they come so close to God and no closer. Jesus, however, as God's Son, knows God without limitations.

God withholds nothing from his own Son. He opens up his very heart to Jesus. He shares his glory with him, he rules his Kingdom with Jesus beside him. The love between the Father and the Son is a private love, a personal and family love, that excludes non-family members. Nobody else is allowed into that private circle, the Holy of Holies.

Jesus is the Heir of God. All that God has belongs to Christ, who can claim it whenever he likes and for whatever reason. God withholds nothing from his Son. God's riches are infinite, and their value can't be measured. Though riches are handed out to God's creation as needed, only the Son has the key to the storehouse. He can and does enjoy the fullness of the richness of God without limit, forever, with "joy unspeakable."

> For in Christ all the fullness of the Deity lives in bodily form. (Colossians 2:9)

God's wisdom and counsel are the very foundation of the universe, of all of God's works both physical and spiritual – and Jesus has full access to them. *He knows the mind of God.* Nothing is hidden from the Son; he is in on the full counsel of God in everything that God does. In fact he is himself the Logos, the wisdom that God used to create the world. Jesus knows the inner workings, the purpose, the value, the dependence and needs, of all Creation as God knows it. He has to, because he too rules over the universe at God's right hand, ruling in wisdom and power. And he is capable of knowing God as he is without limit – which no creature can claim.

Now take all these privileges and *claim them as your own.* This is how you will know God. You will know God through the eyes of Christ, through the body of Christ, through the spiritual senses of Christ. You will know the thoughts of God, as Jesus knows them. Everything that Jesus experiences in Heaven, you will share in.

> All that belongs to the Father is mine. That is why I said the Spirit will take from what is mine and make it known to you. (John 16:15)

> In that day you will no longer ask me anything. I tell you the truth, my Father will give you whatever you ask in my name. Until now you have not asked for anything in my name. Ask and you will receive, and your joy will be complete. (John 16:23-24)

Adam himself didn't have this privilege of knowing God to this extent. He was the pinnacle of creation, and called to be a ruler, but his calling didn't put him by the throne of Heaven! Being the Son of God, Jesus has special privilege that no part of creation can lay claim to. But being the Son of Man, he now includes us in on his high position. *Man can now know the heart and mind of God*, because of what Jesus has done for us.

> I have given them the glory that you gave me, that they may be one as we are one: I in them and you in me. May they be brought to complete unity to let the world know that you sent me and have loved them even as you have loved me. (John 17:22-23)

The other side of this coin is what we are now able to *do* in Christ: we can *love* God as Jesus loves him, and serve and please him as Jesus serves and pleases him. We will have no limitations here either; everything we do for God will be pleasing to him.

> This is my Son, whom I love; with him I am well pleased. (Matthew 3:17)

For eternity past, before the world was ever made, the Father and the Son enjoyed each other. They needed nothing else, and nobody else, because they found their joy and delight in each other. Only the Son knew the Father so well that he could appreciate the fullness of the Father. His inner knowledge of the mind and heart of God enabled him to glory in the Father as the Father deserved to be glorified.

Now we are being let in on that fellowship.

> That which was from the beginning, which we have heard, which we have seen with our eyes, which we have looked at and our hands have touched – this we proclaim concerning the Word of life. The life appeared; we have seen it and testify to it, and we

> proclaim to you the eternal life, which was with the Father and has appeared to us. We proclaim to you what we have seen and heard, so that you also may have fellowship with us. And our fellowship is with the Father and with his Son, Jesus Christ. (1 John 1:1-3)

Jesus brings us so close to the Father that we will see and love what he sees – a privileged view of God that no other creature has ever seen. We are going to touch the depths of God that used to be appreciated and taken advantage of by only Christ himself before time. We will serve God only as Jesus can serve him, being his Son. Angels, for example, will always be mystified about certain aspects of the infinite God, because they won't be let in on the secret of the heart of God. Man is going to know and love these things.

So, Jesus came to lift us up to *his* position in Heaven, so that we can see God as he sees him.

> I am the way and the truth and the life. No one comes to the Father except through me. If you really knew me, you would know my Father as well. From now on, you do know him and have seen him. (John 14:6-7)

> For God, who said, "Let light shine out of darkness," made his light shine in our hearts to give us the light of the knowledge of the glory of God in the face of Christ. (2 Corinthians 4:6)

From this vantage point, we will be able to testify that "truly God *is* good!" Jesus alone knows the depths of the goodness of God, like no one else does. Seeing what he sees in God, our testimony about God's goodness will come from experience, not just hearsay. Then God will get the *full* glory that he deserves for being who he is, since we will be able to personally testify of his fullness.

Heaven

Now the dwelling of God is with men, and he will live with them. They will be his people, and God himself will be with them and be their God. (Revelation 21:3)

We've finally come to the point where we can talk about Heaven.

Probably most people consider Heaven to be a vacation spot, a deserved rest from the cares and troubles of this world, a world full of "good things" that we can enjoy forever. Those same people, however, would have trouble identifying just what those "good things" are! Heaven seems so other-worldly; it's a place that we don't know much about. So, since they don't want to worry about such things needlessly, they put off thinking about Heaven until the time comes to go. But they still want to go there.

And then there are those who think that Heaven is simply an extension of this world's good things. They're hoping to see the same physical pleasures in Heaven that they enjoyed here on earth, only without the limitations and drawbacks. Like a rose without the thorns.

Hopefully you have followed our argument so far, and you realize what Heaven really is. Heaven is being with *God*. In Heaven we are finally going to experience the goodness, the power, the wisdom, the beauty and glory of God without anything getting between us. We will experience God in his purity and fullness.

A chance to touch God

At this point many will turn away from our Gospel. They were hoping for something more "exciting," something that would appeal to their independence and lusts. When Jesus told the Jews about the "true bread" of Heaven, most of them turned away. They didn't want a Heaven like that.

> "I am the living bread that came down from Heaven. If anyone eats of this bread, he will live forever. This bread is my flesh, which I will give for the life of the world." ... From this time many of his disciples turned back and no longer followed him. (John 6:51, 66)

Of course those who haven't seen God yet are going to be disappointed when they hear that Heaven is "only" God. But those who have tasted the goodness of God, in however small a way, will immediately realize the amazing treasure waiting for us there. Nothing else compares with God! The good things that we have experienced in this world were shadows, poor copies, hollow promises that can't compare to the source of all good things. It's like the Israelites tasting the grapes of Canaan before going in; it sure beats life in the desert!

The unique thing about Heaven is that God is going to remove the old creation out of the way so that we can touch him directly, and he will touch us. Such a thing would destroy our bodies as we are now; our minds couldn't handle the direct glory of God. In our present state, we *need* creation in between us and God to protect us; otherwise the experience would kill us. "You cannot see my face, for no one may see me and live." (Exodus 33:20) So, our bodies are going to change to handle the new requirements of Heaven.

> I declare to you, brothers, that flesh and blood cannot inherit the kingdom of God, nor does the perishable inherit the imperishable. Listen, I tell you a mystery: We

will not all sleep, but we will all be changed – in a flash, in the twinkling of an eye, at the last trumpet. For the trumpet will sound, the dead will be raised imperishable, and we will be changed. For the perishable must clothe itself with the imperishable, and the mortal with immortality. (1 Corinthians 15:50-53)

By the way, here is the answer to the old heresy of Gnosticism. The Gnostics believed that the body was sinful, or at best unnecessary to spiritual life. It's a piece of dirt that has to be washed off our souls. It's a burden that has to be thrown off before we can enter Heaven. But they were wrong. God created us physical and he had good reason to do so: that we might enjoy him through our physical senses as well as in our spirits. We are designed to experience God in two ways: through our spirits and through creation blessings.

Heaven is going to be the same way only with a twist. Our spirits will be united with Christ so that we can enjoy God spiritually, but our bodies are going to be *resurrected* so that we can enjoy God's blessings through our senses also. Our bodies (and their physical senses) won't be on the old design; we are going to have a new design so that *through our bodies we can touch God himself.* That's something Adam was never able to do; that's the privilege that Jesus has with his Father right now in Heaven as a man. So, God is going to keep the body, not throw it away. It will be an added means of experiencing him, to the joy and pleasure of man.

A new ruler

God hasn't forgotten the purpose for which he made man.

Let us make man in our image, in our likeness, and let them rule over the fish of the sea and the birds of the

> air, over the livestock, over all the earth, and over all the creatures that move along the ground. (Genesis 1:26)

In fact, I have a feeling that man was destined for great things – if he had behaved himself. But since he rebelled against God, he can't be allowed to spread his rebellion and destruction all over the universe. Earth now is a prison to keep man contained (though we haven't hesitated to trash the planet and each other while we're being held here!) until a solution could be brought in.

Now the solution has come, and God is going to let man out of prison.[4] Through Christ we are cleaned up, restored, lifted up to the level of perfection, made sons of God Most High, and we will sit beside him by his throne. *We have once again become rulers over God's Kingdom.*

We know something about this by the hints that Jesus gave us in the Gospels, and Paul and other Apostles in their letters.

> "Well done, my good servant!" his master replied. "Because you have been trustworthy in a very small matter, take charge of ten cities." (Luke 19:17)

> Do you not know that we will judge angels? (1 Corinthians 6:3)

David, too, provided a model for Christ's Kingdom. When he finally became king over Israel, he appointed his loyal troops to important government positions to help him rule over the land. And he assigned priests their duties in the Temple, to make sure the work of God continued there for the benefit of the people. We already saw this hint of things to come in the passages from Revelation 1:6 and 5:10. What exactly our roles will be, it's hard to say at this point. But we are destined for the throne.

---

[4] Some of us, anyway. God is so angry at the human race in general for slapping him in the face that most of them are going to be destroyed. Many passages of Scripture teach this. The Flood shows us his willingness to do so. See 2 Peter 2:4-9.

Now, just as it required a connection with God for Adam to rule the earth with wisdom, so it will require a deep and profound wisdom for us to rule over the new Heavens and earth. That's why Jesus brings us into such an intimate relationship with God through *him*. We need to know God as the Son of God knows him, so that we can rule as well as Jesus rules.

> The Spirit of the LORD will rest on him – the Spirit of wisdom and of understanding, the Spirit of counsel and of power, the Spirit of knowledge and of the fear of the LORD – and he will delight in the fear of the LORD. He will not judge by what he sees with his eyes, or decide by what he hears with his ears; but with righteousness he will judge the needy, with justice he will give decisions for the poor of the earth. He will strike the earth with the rod of his mouth; with the breath of his lips he will slay the wicked. Righteousness will be his belt and faithfulness the sash around his waist. The wolf will live with the lamb, the leopard will lie down with the goat, the calf and the lion and the yearling together; and a little child will lead them. The cow will feed with the bear, their young will lie down together, and the lion will eat straw like the ox. The infant will play near the hole of the cobra, and the young child put his hand into the viper's nest. They will neither harm nor destroy on all my holy mountain, for the earth will be full of the knowledge of the LORD as the waters cover the sea. (Isaiah 11:2-9)

In Christ's Kingdom there is peace, prosperity, justice, wisdom, balance, *life*. Though we can't possibly imagine it, God's new world will be far and away better than the one we're in now. It will be spiritual, it will be eternal, it will be good without any drawbacks, it will be created in such a way as to show off the glory of God far more powerfully than the present world does. It will take the wisdom of God to rule over it perfectly, with no mistakes. And since we are united with Christ, there will be no mistakes.

The bride of Christ

Just when we thought that there was nothing more that God could possibly bless us with, Jesus tells us about a wedding day coming up. And *we* are the bride.

> The kingdom of Heaven is like a king who prepared a wedding banquet for his son. (Matthew 22:2)

> Christ loved the church and gave himself up for her to make her holy, cleansing her by the washing with water through the Word, and to present her to himself as a radiant church, without stain or wrinkle or any other blemish, but holy and blameless. (Ephesians 5:25-27)

Marriage is the most intimate relationship on earth. Two people come together and know each other, they love each other, they become one. What goes on there is just between them; nobody else has the right to enter into that private zone of pleasure and delight in each other.

The Song of Songs was written to show us how Christ feels about his Church, and how we're going to feel about him. It gets pretty graphic in its details! But it is using marriage as a picture of just how passionate God is about bringing us into his house to live with him. This isn't an intellectual exercise to him. His goal is *intimate* knowledge, knowing things about God that he wouldn't reveal to anybody else. How far short we fall in our ideas of Heaven when we limit it to simply restoring the fallen sinner to the presence of God! Even the angels have that position. We, however, despite how impossible it sounds, are going all the way into his personal chambers. There will be nothing he won't show us about himself. Our relationship with him will be eternal pleasure and delight, on both sides.

Each with a testimony

We are all unique creatures; each creature that God makes is unique. We have characteristics that make us different from everyone else. People often wonder if we'll be able to recognize each other in Heaven! I don't know where they got the idea that they wouldn't. Of course we will know each other. But we're going to be even more unique, even more glorious, even more fully developed than we are now.

This is going to have an interesting aspect in Heaven. Every creature on earth has a story to tell about the goodness of God. Each person too, no matter how anti-God he may be in his heart, also can testify about how God blessed him in *his* life. No story is the same. Now lift that person to Heaven, cleanse him of *his* sins, make *his* mind and heart conform to Christ's image, give him a new body to replace the old one *he* had to suffer with, and we have another unique story about God's mercy and grace. The account that this person will give about God will bring out new and exciting news about who God is and what he did.

Now multiply this by millions upon millions. Can you imagine how thrilling it will be to see the richness of God as he addresses every single individual there in his own needs and growth? Are you looking forward to exploring the depth of that infinite wisdom, the creativity and beauty and power behind all those works of God? Do you have any idea of how long that will take to fully explore and appreciate the wisdom and works of God?

Now swing the picture around to the future, to the eternity that spreads before us. Each one of those individuals with their unique makeup and history will be assigned a place in the new Kingdom that God is building. Each one will have the place exactly suited to their skills. Each one will (as Adam was designed to do) completely depend on God for his wisdom, drawing different resources and power to do their unique task. What is this God like, who can so supply and orchestrate such a vast and complex system with perfect skill, who can create a Paradise that lasts forever?

The glory of Heaven

The glory of Heaven will be this: that God finally will get the credit he deserves. It's been long overdue. Our world is so broken, and we are such rebellious sinners, that very few people are aware of how holy God really is – in other words, how badly they need him alone. But that will change when God destroys this old world and remakes everything on a new plan. There will no longer be a barrier between God and his creation; he will be the very foundation of the world, its power and joy and source of blessing. God's presence will be felt throughout his Kingdom; he will no longer be hidden.

And the children of God are going to have a major role in that new world. Being one with Christ, we will know the depths of God as only Jesus knows him. We've been brought from death to life, from sin to righteousness, from being broken to restoration – in and through Christ. The depths of the heart of God are now clearly seen in what he has done for his children. Our testimony will bring to light a whole new aspect of the holiness of God.

No wonder, then, that in his prayer of John 17, Jesus talks about us sharing in God's glory in Heaven. Glory is actually advertising the holiness of God; it's bringing to light the nature of God. And nobody knows the Father as well as we do now, being so close to him in Christ. As Jesus brought glory to the Father by fully revealing him to us, we also will glorify the Father – and the Son – by revealing what he has done in us. Like the candles in the Temple, we are lights that illuminate the inner recesses of

God's house. What a position that Christ has placed us in! *This*, we will say to the universe, is what God will do for those he delights to honor. We will be clothed with the glory of God, holy and set apart in Christ to know and enjoy the fullness of God, shining with that fullness of God as he lives in us. We will "shine like stars in the universe" (Philippians 2:15), revealing the depths of the love of God. It's this privilege of knowing and revealing the glory of God that Jesus wants us to share in.

> Father, I want those you have given me to be with me where I am, and to see my glory, the glory you have given me because you loved me before the creation of the world. (John 17:24)

> I have made you known to them, and will continue to make you known in order that the love you have for me may be in them and that I myself may be in them. (John 17:26)

God's delight in Heaven will be the fact that we take delight in him as our Father, and live in him alone. *That* is holiness – that God is the center of everything. And Jesus makes it all possible.

Truly …

> From him and through him and to him are all things. To him be the glory forever! Amen. (Romans 11:36)

Eternity will not be enough time to sit at this God's feet in holy wonder.

1 Chronicles 16:8-36

Note how this passage glorifies (makes known, advertises, reveals, takes wonder in) God by bringing out how unique he is, and how much his creatures depend on him for everything. His holiness consists in how he alone is God and can do these amazing things.

Give thanks to the LORD, call on his Name; make known among the nations what he has done. Sing to him, sing praise to him; tell of all his wonderful acts. Glory in his holy Name; let the hearts of those who seek the LORD rejoice.

Look to the LORD and his strength; seek his face always. Remember the wonders he has done, his miracles, and the judgments he pronounced, O descendants of Israel his servant, O sons of Jacob, his chosen ones.

He is the LORD our God; his judgments are in all the earth. He remembers his covenant forever, the word he commanded, for a thousand generations, the covenant he made with Abraham, the oath he swore to Isaac. He confirmed it to Jacob as a decree, to Israel as an everlasting covenant: "To you I will give the land of Canaan as the portion you will inherit."

When they were but few in number, few indeed, and strangers in it, they wandered from nation to nation, from one kingdom to another. He allowed no man to oppress them; for their sake he rebuked kings: "Do not touch my anointed ones; do my prophets no harm."

Sing to the LORD, all the earth; proclaim his salvation day after day. Declare his glory among the nations, his marvelous deeds among all peoples. For great is the LORD and most worthy of praise; he is to be feared above all gods. For all the gods of the nations are idols, but the LORD made the heavens. Splendor and majesty are before him; strength and joy in his dwelling place.

Ascribe to the LORD, O families of nations, ascribe to the LORD glory and strength, ascribe to the LORD the glory due his Name. Bring an offering and come before him; worship the LORD in the splendor of his holiness.

Tremble before him, all the earth! The world is firmly established; it cannot be moved. Let the heavens rejoice, let the earth be glad; let them say among the nations, "The LORD reigns!" Let the sea resound, and all that is in it; let the fields be jubilant, and everything in them! Then the trees of the forest will sing, they will sing for joy before the LORD, for he comes to judge the earth.

Give thanks to the LORD, for he is good; his love endures forever. Cry out, "Save us, O God our Savior; gather us and deliver us from the nations, that we may give thanks to your holy Name, that we may glory in your praise." Praise be to the LORD, the God of Israel, from everlasting to everlasting.

Then all the people said "Amen" and "Praise the LORD."

Edwards' Concept of God's Holiness

Jonathan Edwards

That if God *himself* be, in *any* respect, properly *capable* of being his own end in the creation of the world, then it is reasonable to suppose that he had respect to *himself*, as his last and highest end, in this work; because he is *worthy* in himself to be so, being infinitely the greatest and best of beings. All things else, with regard to worthiness, importance, and excellence, are perfectly as nothing in comparison of him. And therefore, if God has respect to things according to their nature and proportions, he must necessarily have the greatest respect to himself. It would be against the perfection of his nature, his wisdom, holiness, and perfect rectitude, whereby he is disposed to do every thing that is fit to be done, to suppose otherwise. At least, a great part of the moral rectitude of God, whereby he is disposed to every thing that is fit, suitable, and amiable in itself, consists in his having the highest regard to that which is in itself highest and best. The moral rectitude of God must consist in a due respect to things that are objects of moral respect; that is, to intelligent beings capable of moral actions and relations. And therefore it must chiefly consist in giving due respect to that Being to whom most is due; for God is infinitely the most worthy of regard. The worthiness of others is as nothing to his; so that to him belongs all possible respect. To him belongs the *whole* of the respect that any intelligent being is capable of. To him belongs all the heart. Therefore, if moral rectitude of heart consists in paying the respect of the heart which is due, or which fitness and suitableness requires, fitness requires infinitely the greatest regard to be paid to God; and the denying of supreme regard here would be a conduct infinitely the most unfit. Hence it will follow, that the moral rectitude of the disposition, inclination, or affection of God chiefly consists in a regard to himself, infinitely above his regard to all other beings; or, in other words, **his holiness consists in this**. (*Emphasis is the editor's.*)

And if it be thus fit that God should *have* a supreme regard to himself, then it is fit that this supreme regard should *appear* in those things by which he makes himself known, or by his *word* and *works*, *i.e.* in what he *says*, and in what he *does*. If it be an infinitely amiable thing in God, that he should have a supreme regard to himself, then it is an amiable thing that he should *act* as having a chief regard to himself; or act in such a manner, as to *show* that he has such a regard: that what is highest in God's *heart*, may be highest in his *actions* and *conduct*. And if it was God's intention, as there is great reason to think it was, that his *works* should exhibit an *image* of himself their author, that it might brightly appear by his works what manner of being he is, and afford a proper representation of his divine excellencies, and especially his *moral* excellence, consisting in the *disposition of his heart*; then it is reasonable to suppose that his works are so wrought as to *show* this supreme respect to himself, wherein his moral excellence primarily consists.

Taken from ***A Dissertation on the End for which God Created the World,*** *in* ***The Works of Jonathan Edwards****, Vol. 1, pp. 97-98.* ***Banner of Truth Trust***: 1974 Edition

For an in-depth discussion on Creation, see:

The Bible Explains Creation

For a description of the Covenant given to Abraham, see:

Ten Keys to the Bible

For an analysis of David's kingdom and Christ's use of that plan in constructing his church, see:

The Throne of David

For putting together a hermeneutic for interpreting the Old and New Testaments, see:

A New Model for Biblical Studies

These titles are available from ***Ravenbrook Publishers****. You can order them and other titles on-line at* **www.shenbible.org** *or you can find them at your local bookstore.*

Notes

www.ingramcontent.com/pod-product-compliance
Lightning Source LLC
LaVergne TN
LVHW091008080826
845145LV00003B/1171

9780615156194